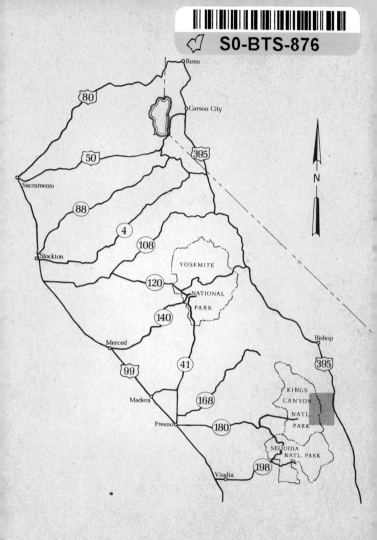

Location of the MT. PINCHOT quadrangle

Kearsarge Pinnacles

High Sierra
Hiking Guide #14

Mt. Pinchot

by John W. Robinson

with the editors of
WILDERNESS PRESS
Thomas Winnett
editor-in-chief

Photos by the author
except as noted

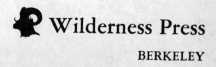

Wilderness Press

BERKELEY

Acknowledgments

Numerous individuals contributed time and effort toward the completion of this guide. The writer is indebted to them for their friendly counsel and advice, which made my task easier and more pleasant. My friend Andrew Smatko, coeditor of *Mountaineer's Guide to the High Sierra*, provided valuable information on cross-country routes. Jim Jenkins, Tom Amneus and Joe McCosker were my companions on many scouting trips into the *Mt. Pinchot* country. The rangers of Kings Canyon National Park and Inyo National Forest were always cooperative and willing to endure and answer my many questions. Jeff Schaffer contributed his geological expertise and completed the accompanying topographical map. Last but not least, Thomas Winnett, editor-in-chief of Wilderness Press, contributed his usual wise counsel and gave overall guidance to the project. To these, and to many others who aided in smaller but important ways, my deep gratitude.

John W. Robinson
Costa Mesa, California
November 6, 1973

Introduction

The HIGH SIERRA HIKING GUIDES by the editors of Wilderness Press are the first *complete* guides to the famous High Sierra. Most guides cover one 15-minute U.S.G.S. topographic quadrangle, which is an area about 14 miles east-west by 17 miles north-south. This is a complete guide to the *Mt. Pinchot* quadrangle, covering the southeastern section of Kings Canyon National Park and a good part of the John Muir Wilderness in Inyo National Forest. The inside front cover shows the location of the area covered by this guide.

There is a great and increasing demand for literature about America's favorite wilderness, John Muir's "Range of Light." To meet this demand, we have undertaken this guide series. The purpose of each book in the series is threefold: first, to provide a reliable basis for planning a trip; second, to serve as a field guide while you are on the trail; and third, to stimulate you to further field investigation and background reading. In each guide, there are a minimum of 100 described miles of trails, and the descriptions are supplemented with maps and other logistical and background information. HIGH SIERRA HIKING GUIDES are based on firsthand observation. There is absolutely no substitute for walking the trails, so we walked all the trails.

In planning this series, we chose the 15-minute quadrangle as the unit because—though every way of dividing the Sierra is arbitrary—the topographic quadrangle map (topo map) is the chosen aid of almost every wilderness traveler. Inside the back cover of this book is a map of the quadrangle, showing described trails and good campsites. With this map, you can always get where you want to go, with a minimum of detours or wasted effort.

One other thing the wilderness traveler will need: a permit from the Forest Service (for federally designated wilderness areas) or from the National Park Service (for national-park backcountry). You may obtain a permit at a Park Service or Forest Service ranger station or office by indicating where you are going and when you will be there. The Forest Service requires a permit for a day hike as well as a backpack. The two services will reciprocally honor each other's permits for trips that cross a boundary between the two types of wilderness. The Forest Service permits are also available by mail. If you don't know the address of the nearest Forest Service office or station, write the Regional Forester, 630 Sansome St., San Francisco, Calif. 94111.

Table of Contents

The Country

THE *MT. PINCHOT* COUNTRY represents the High Sierra at its finest. The hiker rambling southward along the John Muir Trail discovers this as he passes through some of the most dramatic stretches of high alpine wilderness in the West. To his left soar the stark crags and jagged ridgelines of the main crest, a twisted, multicolored blending of granitic and metamorphic rocks. Sparkling sky-blue lakes are set like precious jewels in glaciated bedrock, and often bordered with flower-bedecked meadows. Trees are tortured and dwarfed at timberline, but superbly tall in the forests below. Snowfields cling stubbornly to north-facing slopes well into summer, nourishing ribbons of churning white water that, once released from its frozen state, hurries westward. The air is thin and crisp with the chill of elevation. Nights are cold, but the midday sun is bedazzling, and it quickly leaves the brush of sunburn on the unprotected lowlander. This is truly a land of primeval grandeur.

The mighty Sierra crest snakes through the middle of this high mountain region, separating two slopes that are as different as night and day. Westward, the tilt is gradual as the 12,000- and 13,000-foot summits recede into high basins, spotted with lakes and ponds that serve as spawning grounds for one of the Sierra's major watersheds—the South Fork of the Kings and its major tributaries, Woods and Bubbs creeks. All three of these watercourses, rushing essentially west and southwest, have, through eons of time, carved deep gorges into the granite bedrock. Some of the most sublime scenery in the range is found along trails that follow two of these great canyons—Woods Creek and Bubbs Creek. The South Fork of the Kings has scenery of equal grandeur, but the route through most of this chasm is trailless.

Eastward from the crest, the contrast is startling. The mighty Sierra rampart plunges in castellated ridges and sheer cliffs to the sage-covered floor of Owens Valley, losing 8000 feet of elevation in four or five horizontal miles, and forming the most awesome continuous mountain wall in the continental United States. Trails climb this eastern face and cross the crest in four places in the *Mt. Pinchot* quadrangle—Taboose Pass, Sawmill Pass, Baxter Pass and Kearsarge Pass. Of the four, only Kearsarge Pass is recommended for the beginner— this because one gets a "head start" at Onion Valley. The other three trails require long, steep, exhausting ascents from the desert floor, through the realm of bighorn sheep and Inyo mule deer.

This *Mt. Pinchot* country holds appeal for all who enter. The hiker will be delighted to stroll along some of the most scenic, well-maintained trails in the Sierra, and savor some fine cross-country routes also. The fisherman will enjoy trying his skills at the beautiful Rae Lakes or in Sixty Lake Basin, where angling, depending on the season, is good to excellent. The climber can test his ability on the granite walls of Mt. Clarence King, along the knife edge of Mt. Gardiner, or on the blackish slabs of Dragon Peak. The camper who is packed in over Kearsarge Pass will appreciate the sublime charm of the Kearsarge Lakes or Charlotte Lake.

Fortunately, almost all of *Mt. Pinchot* country is protected for future generations to enjoy. The region west of the crest is encompassed within Kings Canyon National Park. East of the crest is the John Muir Wilderness, administered by Inyo

National Forest. Despite this wilderness status, heavy use—particularly in the Onion Valley/Kearsarge Pass and Rae Lakes areas—poses a serious threat to the natural beauty of the region. The National Park Service and the Forest Service have found it necessary to restrict camping and grazing. Visitors to *Mt. Pinchot* country need to be conservation-minded, taking nothing but pictures, leaving nothing but footprints.

Words are no substitute for a real wilderness experience in this superb mountain sanctuary. Come on foot, with receptive mind and heart, and rejoice as Muir did a century ago, "bathing in its glorious floods of light, seeing the sunbursts of morning among the icy peaks, the noonday radiance on the trees and rocks and snow, the flush of alpenglow, and a thousand dashing waterfalls with their marvelous abundance of irised spray." You will understand why Muir called the Sierra the "Range of Light."

Fin Dome over Dollar Lake

The History

THE EARLIEST PEOPLE known to have visited the *Mt. Pinchot* country were the Paiute Indians of Owens Valley. Just how long ago these hardy Indian people penetrated this region is uncertain, but it was at least three or four centuries before the appearance of the white man. The hunting of game and the gathering of food occupied the major attention of the Paiutes. To obtain this livelihood, these Indians penetrated well into the eastern Sierra Nevada. Here, mainly on the lower slopes and in the canyons, they found pinyon nuts, various types of edible seeds, and animals—deer, rabbits, birds and fish—enough to satisfy their needs. In summer, to escape from the searing desert heat of Owens Valley, whole villages moved up into the cool heights of the Sierra.

Indian trading routes crossed the Sierra crest via both Taboose and Kearsarge passes. From the Yokuts in the western foothills of the range, the Paiutes received deer skins and baskets, which were usually paid for with obsidian, gathered in the desert ranges and highly valued for making tools and weapons. Obsidian arrowheads are still occasionally found in *Mt. Pinchot* country.

Probably the first white men to view this high mountain region were the men of the Joseph Walker party who trekked north through Owens Valley during the spring of 1834. Intent upon returning to Salt Lake as quickly as possible, Walker and his lieutenant Zenas Leonard, who kept a diary that is of great value to historians, made only perfunctory note of the lofty mountain crest they passed under. Walker traversed Owens Valley again in 1843, leading one of John C. Fremont's

---

Shorty Lovelace's cabin on Woods Creek

parties, but once more he took no special interest in the mountains.

Many other pioneers passed through Owens Valley in the 1840s and 1850s and must have gazed at the steel-gray rampart on the western skyline, perhaps wondering whether this formidable barrier could be surmounted. As far as is known today, the first crossing by a white man of this rampart in the *Mt. Pinchot* quadrangle occurred in 1858. Inyo County historian W.A. Chalfant relates the facts: "During the summer of 1858 a Tulare man named J.H. Johnson and five comrades were piloted across Kearsarge Pass by a Digger Indian named Sampson. . . . When Johnson and his party reached this slope [Owens Valley] the Paiutes were found to be hostile, and two Indians were killed in a skirmish." It is not known whether Johnson and his friends returned via the same route. In any event, the old Kearsarge Pass Indian trail became known to white settlers on both sides of the Sierra, and it was frequently used after that.

The first to scientifically investigate and explore the *Mt. Pinchot* country were the intrepid men of the famous Whitney Survey party—William H. Brewer, Clarence King, James Gardiner, Richard Cotter and Charles Hoffman. The party entered the Sierra via the Kings River and its South Fork in June 1864. The challenge of uncharted peaks and deep canyons laced with rushing rivers were the magnets that drew them deep into the heart of the range. After climbing Mt. Brewer to learn the pattern of the land, they worked their way painstakingly up toward the headwaters of the South Fork, marveling at the colossal granite cliffs and gorging themselves on trout. They hoped to continue north to Mt. Goddard but failed to find a route negotiable by their pack animals. Instead, they retraced their steps and turned east, crossed the Sierra crest via Kearsarge Pass and descended into Owens Valley. In retrospect, the Brewer party's explorations in the summer of 1864, covering the High Sierra from Yosemite to the Kern River, rank among the most notable exploits in the history of the Sierra Nevada. Three of the men—King, Gardiner and Cotter—have peaks named for them in the *Mt. Pinchot* quadrangle.

The discovery and development of Nevada's fabulous Comstock Lode encouraged prospectors to search elsewhere east of the Sierra for mineral riches. Miners entered Owens Valley in the early 1860s and uncovered a number of promising veins in the desert ranges east of the valley. To fuel the kilns, shore up tunnels and build mining towns, woodcutters reached into the Sierra for timber. Today, such place-names as Shingle Mill Bench and Sawmill Canyon commemorate these wood-gathering activities of the past.

While cutting timber above Little Pine Creek (now Independence Creek) in late spring of 1864, woodcutters discovered quartz veins rich in gold and silver. Prospectors immediately rushed to this east slope of the Sierra. They called their first mine Kearsarge in honor of the Union battleship that had recently sunk the Confederate raider *Alabama*. That would show the Confederate sympathizers down in the hills east of Lone Pine who had named their claims Alabama! The ramshackle town of Kearsarge hastily appeared along the creek just below Onion Valley, and the Kearsarge Mining District was organized, extending along the east face of the Sierra from the Alabama Hills to Big Pine Creek. Prospects looked incredibly rich at first. One ore shipment, sent to Nevada for milling, netted over $900 to the ton.

Development of various claims along the slopes of Kearsarge Peak continued through 1865 and 1866, even though work had to be suspended for weeks during winter because of heavy snows. Some $40,000 was spent erecting the 10-stamp Kearsarge Mill just below the diggings. Three of the mines became the top producers: the *Silver Spout*, at 11,500 feet just south of the summit of Kearsarge Peak; the *Rex Montis*, highest of the mines, at 12,000 feet on the north side of the peak's east shoulder; and the original *Kearsarge*, at 9000 feet on the southeast flank of the mountain.

The winter of 1866-67 was unusually severe. Most of the miners departed the town of Kearsarge for the warmer valley below, but some remained holed up in their cabins. On the afternoon of March 1, 1867, calamity struck with deadly swiftness. A mammoth avalanche thundered down the mountainside and completely demolished the town of Kearsarge, snuffing out the lives of all but a handful of those who had remained. The old mining camp never recovered.

Work continued on the Kearsarge claims, off and on for many years, but the profits never lived up to initial expectations. Operating difficulties, made worse by the high, rugged terrain, proved too great an obstacle. Repeated attempts were made, as late as 1935, to make the mines pay, but all met with failure. Today, the fading remnants of this century-old operation can be viewed on the mountainside as one drives up the new highway to Onion Valley.

The first to exploit *Mt. Pinchot* country west of the Sierra crest were sheepmen. Herdsmen brought armies of "hoofed locusts" well up the South Fork of the Kings River as early as 1875. Taboose, Sawmill and Pinchot passes were crossed by sheepmen before 1890. In some areas, emerald meadows turned into barren fields of dust, ruined by the sharp hooves and ravenous appetites of these wool-bearing animals. Fortunately, the worst was over by 1890, when falling wool prices lowered the incentive to raise sheep. The final blow to sheepmen was the prohibition of sheep from the great Sierra Forest Reserve set aside by President Benjamin Harrison in 1893, thanks largely to the conservation voices of men like John Muir, Robert Underwood and George Stewart.

The period from 1864 until shortly after the turn of the century was one of exploration of the High Sierra, beginning with the famed Brewer party's travels. In 1868 Judge Elisha C. Winchell of Fresno explored the Kings River region and entered the southwestern section of *Mt. Pinchot* country. Lil A. Winchell, the judge's son, continued the family explorations in the late 1870s. John Muir came south from Yosemite in 1873, traveling up Bubbs Creek and over Kearsarge Pass. He returned to the region in 1875. Muir was the first to proclaim the esthetic glories of the Sierra. Stanford professor Bolton Coit Brown made a solo trip up the Muro Blanco to the headwaters of the South Fork of the Kings in 1895, making first ascents of Mt. Ruskin and Arrow Peak and mapping the area. He returned with his wife, Lucy, the following year, met the party of Joseph N. Le Conte, and with him ascended Bubbs and Charlotte creeks and made the first ascent of Mt. Gardiner.

This trip, along with other excursions made during the previous decade, stimulated interest in a high route along the backbone of the Sierra. Theodore S. Solomons, who conceived

and publicized the idea of a high route in the 1890s, has
been called the father of the John Muir Trail. In 1914 the
Sierra Club formed a committee to enlist the help and coopera-
tion of the State of California in the construction of this pro-
posed pathway. Soon thereafter John Muir, president of the
Sierra Club, died, and it was decided to name the new route
"The John Muir Trail" as a fitting memorial. As a result of the
committee's efforts, the California Legislature appropriated
$10,000 to finance work on the trail in 1915. Additional ap-
propriations were made by the Legislature in ensuing years.
The US Forest Service handled most of the actual construction
of the trail, which required more than two decades to complete. The final section—over Mather Pass to the headwaters
of the South Fork of the Kings—was completed in 1938. Since
then, thousands each summer have savored the delights of this
wilderness footpath.

Mt. Pinchot country from the Sierra crest westward became
part of Kings Canyon National Park when the Park was created
on March 4, 1940. In 1964 the region immediately east of the
crest was proclaimed the John Muir Wilderness of Inyo National Forest. All of the magnificent High Sierra country in
the *Mt. Pinchot* quadrangle is now preserved in wilderness
form for the enjoyment of present and future generations.
However, increasing numbers of backpackers visit the *Mt.
Pinchot* region every summer, making it difficult to maintain
the primeval aspects of the mountains. For this reason the
National Park Service is now limiting the number of visitors
who may enter the area at any one time. Only by the applica-
tion of such stringent measures will the High Sierra continue
to hold its wilderness appeal.

The Geology

THE SIERRA, OWENS VALley and the basin ranges to the east represent great blocks that have buckled and tilted in much the same manner as would a poorly laid cement walk. By far the most massive of these blocks is the Sierra itself. The range can be compared to a mammoth door lying in a horizontal position and slightly ajar. Its hinges lie buried under sediments in the Central Valley of California, while its open, eastern edge—the Sierra crest— rises to elevations of 13,000 and 14,000 feet. Riding piggyback atop this uplifted and tilted segment of the crust are the remnants of ancestral ranges which, exposed to forces over a long period, were extensively warped and faulted. East from the crest, the Sierra drops in stupendous fashion to the depressed floor of the Owens Valley.

Nowhere is the Sierra's eastern escarpment more awesome and abrupt than in the area covered by the *Mt. Pinchot* and *Mt. Whitney* quadrangles. Unlike much of the Sierra crest farther north, no intervening hills or ridges soften the plunge from alpine summit to desert floor. This is mountain country of extremely high relief. The elevation difference within the *Mt. Pinchot* quadrangle is almost 10,000 feet, ranging from a low of 3860 feet in Owens Valley to the 13,495-foot crown of Mt. Pinchot. In spite of this great difference, more than half of the area of the quadrangle lies above an elevation of 9000 feet. The general slope west from the crest is much more gradual than the steep eastern scarp. However, stream carving and glaciation have produced a boldly sculptured and deeply creased topography that gives this part of the High Sierra a sublime alpine appearance.

How was all this created? It has been said that the story of the earth is written in the rocks, and this is certainly evident in the *Mt. Pinchot* country. Since most of the surface of the quadrangle is sparsely vegetated or above timberline, its highly diversified rock formations lie exposed to anyone who might want to reconstruct the area's geologic history.

During most of the Paleozoic era—approximately 570 million to 230 million years before present (B.P.)—the *Mt. Pinchot* region was a shallow sea bed or a coastal lowland. Sediments accumulated to depths of thousands of feet over this long period, but today they are too deformed and piecemeal to permit a detailed interpretation of the ancient, Paleozoic landscapes. The original sediments were mudstone, siltstone, shale and limestone, but these were later metamorphosed—changed by heat and pressure—into schist, hornfels and, to a lesser extent, marble. Today, geologists call these ancient rocks "Paleozoic metasedimentary formations"—*meta* meaning "changed." In the Sierra they are oriented in a northwest-southeast direction, extending discontinuously from the northeastern part of the *Mt. Pinchot* quadrangle northwest to southeastern Yosemite National Park. You can see outcroppings of Paleozoic schist just west of Taboose Pass and along the Muir Trail near Twin Lakes. Immediately below Sawmill Lake is a fine example of Paleozoic hornfels.

The Mesozoic era—extending from about 230 million to 67 million B.P.—was a period of intense deformation within the Sierra. The earth's large crustal plates are known to have been in movement at least from the beginning of this era onward, and the pressures they exerted are apparent in the Sierra's Mesozoic rocks. These pressures warped, folded and faulted the ancient rocks of the *Mt. Pinchot* quadrangle. Periods of intense volcanic activity were followed by intrusions of huge molten granitic masses, called "plutons," which bubbled upward from deep within the crust. The largest single body of metamorphic rock in the quadrangle is a Mesozoic metavolcanic formation—lava and other volcanic deposits that were metamorphosed—about two miles wide and six miles long, extending from just west of the Sierra crest near Baxter Pass southeast to the lower slopes of Kearsarge Peak, encompassing essentially the upper drainage basin of Oak Creek. Slivers of metavolcanic rock can be seen just east of Sawmill Pass and along the eastern base of the range north and south of Independence Creek. The largest preserved remnant of Mesozoic volcanic activity west of the crest is the metarhyolite tuff on Mt. Bago, south of Charlotte Lake.

Most people think of the Sierra as consisting of one great mass of granite, but in fact twenty-seven separate Mesozoic plutons have been mapped in the *Mt. Pinchot* quadrangle. These range in composition from pale silica-rich alaskite to dark-hued, silica-poor gabbro and related rocks. Most of the plutonic rocks are the intermediates quartz monzonite and granodiorite, which are seen along most of the length of the John Muir Trail in the *Mt. Pinchot* region. From Upper Basin to Lake Marjorie you cross a mass of Lamarck granodiorite, which contrasts with the lighter-colored quartz monzonite of the Cartridge Pass pluton visible immediately to the southwest. Around Pinchot Pass and for a short distance south, you walk over dark granodiorite of the McDoogle pluton. Just below Twin Lakes the trail crosses an area of light-colored alaskite, the Twin Lakes pluton. On your way down Woods Creek, you

cross the heavily diked, sheared granitic rocks of the White Fork
pluton and, near Castle Domes, a pluton of alaskite. As the
Muir Trail climbs to Rae Lakes, it enters an extensive region of
dark-hued granodiorite found within the Dragon pluton. Once
over Glen Pass, you abruptly enter the domain of the Bullfrog
pluton, a large, light-colored mass of alaskite that extends the
rest of the way to Vidette Meadow and on out of the quadrangle. Together, the Mesozoic granitic intrusions occupy most
of the *Mt. Pinchot* quadrangle west of the crest.

During much of the early Cenozoic era—an era extending
from about 67 million B.P. to the present –the ancestral Sierra
Nevada was relatively stable, and its crest was probably less
than 5000 feet in elevation. Then, commencing a few million
years ago, major new uplifts occurred in the *Mt. Pinchot* quadrangle as elsewhere in the range, accompanied by westward tilt-
ing and faulting. Most of this uplift, which raised the Sierra
crest to approximately its present elevation, occurred during
the Pleistocene epoch, commencing about two million years
ago, and it was accompanied by sporadic volcanic activity.
This comparatively recent volcanic action can be seen in the
numerous cinder cones and lava flows along the foot of the
Sierra in the *Mt. Pinchot* quadrangle. Young basalt flows are
clearly visible on the lower slopes of Goodale, Division and
Sawmill creeks. Quite interesting are the remnants of a basalt
flow in Sawmill Canyon, which originated from a vent on the
north slope of the canyon at an elevation of 7600 feet, descended the canyon and buried its entrance to a depth of 150
feet. Most of the lower flow has been eroded away by the
creek, but along the trail near The Hogsback, you can still find
spindle-shaped volcanic "bombs" one or two feet long, formed

when molten lava was hurled into the air and solidified while falling.

As the Sierra Nevada was rising in elevation, there was a widespread cooling of the earth's climate. The added elevation intensified the cooling effect. These changes led to a net yearly accumulation of snow, until the entire summit region of the range was profoundly snowbound. Mighty glaciers sculptured the high landscape, gouged out hanging cirques and basins, and sent huge tongues of ice down the canyons of the west slope. The great U-shaped gorges of the *Mt. Pinchot* region—Bubbs Creek, Woods Creek and the South Fork of the Kings—were broadened and deepened to their present shapes during the several glacial epochs in the Sierra. Glaciers also descended the eastside canyons to the floor of Owens Valley, leaving moraines that are still clearly evident. The Hogsback in Sawmill Canyon is an eroded lateral moraine from the last glacial period, and small moraines are preserved near the mouths of Goodale, Oak and Independence creeks.

The last major glaciation ended about 10,000 years ago, and all the Sierra glaciers completely disappeared about 4000 years later, during a warm period. Since then there have been several minor glacial stages, the last one being the "little ice age" of the 16th and 17th centuries. The few small glaciers that cling to high northeast-facing walls along the crest today—most notably the one on the north face of University Peak—are remnants from this age.

The Sierra landscape continues to undergo change. Geologists believe that the range is rising a few inches per century—but its crest is also being attacked by ice, water and wind. Water seeping into minute cracks and turning to ice is steadily eroding and exfoliating the seemingly invincible granite. Mountain walls are gradually crumbling into talus. Streams are cutting deeper channels into bedrock and carrying alluvium down from the heights. The forces of earth and sky are eternally at work.

Upper Basin   *Tom Ross*

The Fauna

THE MIGHTY SIERRA CREST acts as an effective barrier and natural boundary between the life forms—both floral and faunal—of the western and eastern slopes. A surprisingly large number of animal and plant species dwell exclusively on one side or the other. Not only is the jagged crest an imposing physical barrier, but, more important, it is a climatic boundary. Pacific storms empty most of their water on the windward slope, leaving little moisture for the leeward side of the range.

Other books in this series—including the author's companion volume on the *Mt. Goddard* and *Big Pine* quadrangles—have dealt with the life forms west of the Sierra backbone. Here we describe wildlife you are likely to encounter on the abrupt desert-facing slope of the range, from the arid foothills bordering Owens Valley to the 13,000-foot ridges and spires of the crest. Here, as elsewhere, animal life has too often suffered from the carelessness and greed of human visitors. Fortunately, attempts are being made today to preserve these endangered life forms. History makes it unmistakably clear that their fate rests largely in man's stewardship of the land.

Hikers trudging up the long trails to Baxter and Sawmill passes may spot, scampering across the cliffs high above, small herds of bighorn sheep (*Ovis canadensis californiana*). These agile rock climbers have been fittingly called "statuesque masters of the airy crags." They live almost exclusively on the rugged slopes and cliffs east of the crest, avoiding the seemingly more hospitable country to the west. Bighorn sheep are poor runners on gentle terrain, but on rocks they can easily outmaneuver their enemies—mountain lions and men.

Bighorn sheep are readily identifiable by their gray or buffy-brown coat and large, whitish rump patch. Their distinctive horns spiral back and outward, often forming a full circle on males. On females the horns are small and erect, usually with a slight backward curve.

The sheep feed on various species of grasses, sedges and roots found on the eastern Sierra slope. They summer in the alpine heights, and descend in late autumn to the foothill regions 5000 feet below. Soon after their descent, the breeding season begins. The rams battle for possession of bands of ewes, and the clash of horns can be heard from a mile away as the big males rear and charge each other, colliding head-on with their massive horns again and again until one of the rivals has had enough. Mating commences soon after the rivalries are resolved. Gestation takes about six months, and the new lambs appear in May or June, just in time to be escorted back to the heights for the summer season.

Bighorn sheep once lived throughout the eastern Sierra from Sonora Pass to Mt. Langley. But they were reduced by hunting, overgrazing and disease picked up from domestic sheep, until their population is estimated today to be under four hundred, split among several herds in the eastern *Mt. Pinchot* and *Mt. Whitney* quadrangles. To save these noble animals from extinction, the Forest Service in 1972 created two California Bighorn Sheep Zoological Areas along the eastern slope of the Sierra. The Mt. Baxter Zoological Area extends from the summit of Mt. Perkins south to Dragon Peak. From University Peak south to Tunnabora Peak in the *Mt. Whitney* quadrangle is the Mt. Williamson Zoological Area. The higher part of each area is closed to human entry from

June 1 to October 1, when the bighorn sheep herds are dwelling in the high country, and the lower part is closed from December 15 to June 1. An exception is that one may use the Baxter, Sawmill and Shepherd Pass trails all year. In this way, it is hoped, the downward population trend of these animals can be reversed. Only time will tell.

Below the range of the bighorn sheep is the domain of the tule elk (*Cervus canadensis*). This smallest species of American elk is light brown on the body, with darker brown on the neck and legs, and a whitish rump patch. In a migration pattern almost the reverse of bighorn sheep, some of the Owens Valley herd of tule elk move into the Sierra in winter, climbing to about 8000 feet, and return to the valley in spring. They feed on bitterbrush, sage, willow, sedges and grasses. Their mating season is from mid-August through September, when the older bulls each select a harem and defend it against rivals by fighting with their antlers and front hooves. The call, or bugle, of the male tule elk can be heard for long distances. Calves are born in April or May, spotted at birth but losing their spots within two or three months.

Hardly an animal species in the Western Hemisphere has had such a colorful and near-tragic history as the tule elk. They once occurred in numbers that "darkened" the Central Valley of California, their native habitat. From gold-rush days onward, ranchers and hunters killed the elk until, by the 1870s, they were on the brink of extinction. By good fortune, a remnant of the race remained, hiding out in the tules near the southern end of the valley. In 1933 and 1934, 55 tule elk were transplanted to Owens Valley by the California Department of Fish and Game. Here, feeding on the lush grasses and

brush of the valley floor and the Sierra foothills, the elk
thrived. Their numbers reached an estimated 300 by 1955.
But as the herd grew, so did the protests from Owens Valley
cattlemen who claimed that the elk were competing for their
cattle feed and breaking down fences. To appease the ranchers,
the Department of Fish and Game authorized several hunts to
limit the elk herd to less than 200 animals. Alarmed at this
threat to an endangered species, a citizens' group—the Committee for the Preservation of the Tule Elk—was formed in
1960 to press for a larger number. The committee was in-
strumental in persuading the California Fish and Game Com-
mission to raise the tule-elk herd to 250-300 animals. Today,
these graceful animals, protected by law, roam *Mt. Pinchot*
country from the desert floor well up into the eastern Sierra
foothills, complementing their distant relative, the bighorn
sheep.

A close cousin of the California mule deer, dweller of the
Sierra's western slopes, is the Inyo mule deer (*Odocoileus
hemionus inyoensis*), found on the eastern flank of the range.
It takes a trained eye to detect the difference between the two
species. Both are grayish brown with a black-and-white tail,
but the Inyo mule deer has a slight yellowish tinge to its coat,
and its white tail markings are a bit more restrictive. The Inyo
deer spend the winter in the low eastern foothills, then move
up toward the crest in spring, and remain in the high country
until driven back down by snow in October or November. Although they share the same range with bighorn sheep, the two
species are not compatible and give each other a wide berth.

The Flora

THE CROWNING GLORY OF the High Sierra, well exemplified in *Mt. Pinchot* country, is the land above the trees. This is a solitary world of granite and space and distances that are deceiving. There is nothing between you and the sky, no tree branches, no filtering haze, no murky pollution. Faraway peaks are sharp in outline and seem much closer than they are. Snow patches from last winter's storms lie in sheltered nooks. Lakes are sparkling blue and transparent. Most of all, this is a world of luminescence. There is twice as much ultraviolet radiation and twenty-five percent more light than at sea level. It is as if the mountains were illuminated by an inner radiance, capturing the essence of John Muir's epithet, the "Range of Light." Nightfall brings an abrupt change, as subfreezing temperatures permeate everything.

From a distance, this stark tundra country appears barren and lifeless. But this is an illusion. Upon close inspection, grasses, sedges and a multiplicity of flowering plants are seen to spot the rocky terrain, hugging the ground and hiding under boulders. Most of these alpine plants are perennials, blooming year after year from the same sturdy roots. The growing season is too short to allow time for more than a handful of quick-cycling annuals to produce seeds for perpetuating themselves. All the plants have adapted in some way to the harsh environment. They counter the omnipresent wind by growing as low mats and huddling in sheltered cracks. They defeat the intense nighttime cold by trapping daylight heat with such thick and closely knit foliage that the interiors of some of the plant clusters are twenty degrees warmer than the surrounding air. They resist dehydration from the intense solar radiation by producing leaves that are small, leathery or waxy, and covered with fuzz or hairs. Deep, spreading rootstalks store food and water. Between the chinks of all this protective armor sprout delicate flowers of multicolored beauty. Appearing almost frivolous in this stark and hostile landscape, they are a poignant tribute to the tenacity of life, a delight to the few hardy hikers who behold them.

One of Muir's favorites, often called the hiker's flower, is Sierra primrose (*Primula suffrutescens*). This minute, deep-pink flower, springing from a shiny rosette of evergreen leaves, frequents rocky ledges and slopes up to 13,500 feet, sometimes appearing to be a rosy stain on the granite when viewed from a distance. Most alpine flowers are scattered, but primroses are often so massed as to produce a vivid splash of color on otherwise barren cliffs.

Another member of the primrose family is shooting star (*Dodecatheon Jeffreyi*), its distinctive, streamlined form ranging in color from magenta to lavender, with a maroon ring at its base. This delightful flower is most often found along creeks and in wet patches up to 11,000 feet.

Best known to the mountain climber, and often blooming where there are no other plants, is polemonium, or sky pilot (*Polemonium eximium*). This hardy but dainty dweller of the airy crags raises clusters of light-blue phloxlike blossoms where common sense tells one that no living thing should exist.

A cream-colored, long-spurred gem of the high mountains is columbine (*Aquilegia pubescens*), found on rocky slopes up to 12,000 feet. Its bright blossoms attract hummingbirds and bees because of the abundance of nectar in its hollow spurs.

Dotting the drier slopes and basins of this above-timberline world is alpine phlox (*Phlox caespitosa*), its minute, starlike white flowers rising from conspicuous mats of prickly green foliage. Phlox is commonly found in gravelly and bouldery areas up to 11,500 feet.

A pale-yellow flower that resembles a strawberry blossom in shape is cinquefoil (*Potentilla Breweri*). Many of its stems stand two to three feet high, making its splash of yellow conspicuous against the gray granite.

Alpine laurel (*Kalmia polifolia*) sometimes throws a ring of pink or rosy-purple blossoms around meadows and bogs up to 12,000 feet.

Red mountain heather (*Phyllodoce Breweri*), its small, roundish flowers emerging from dense evergreen foliage, is a familiar sight around timberline tarns and in swampy areas, often a complement to alpine laurel.

White heather (*Cassiope Mertensiana*) clusters on rocky ridges and under ledges, densely matted. Its bell-shaped flowers, white or slightly pinkish, are among the most beautiful of alpine floral delights. The sight of white heather prompted John Muir to write: "Here . . . I met Cassiope growing in fringes among the battered rocks. . . . Her blossoms had faded long ago, but they were still clinging with happy memories to the evergreen sprays, and still so beautiful as to thrill every fiber of one's being. Winter and summer you may hear her voice, the low sweet melody of her bells. No evangel among all the mountain plants speaks Nature's love more plainly than Cassiope."

The hiker who becomes familiar with this high-altitude flora will find his wilderness experience markedly enriched.

The Climate

JOHN MUIR REJOICED IN the ineffable beauty and harmony of a Sierra thunderstorm. To this great naturalist, it was a glorious experience to be outside during nature's tempest and to feel "the rush and roar and ecstasy of motion—air and lightning and water and the mighty mountains rejoicing in their strength and singing in harmony." His journals contain accounts of his hurrying up ridges and climbing to the uppermost branches of forest monarchs in order to witness more fully the fury of wind, lightning and rain.

Muir apparently never gave second thought to the perils of lightning. Perhaps, were he alive today and made aware of the three dozen or so deaths and injuries that occur annually from lightning strikes, he might not be so eager to expose himself on rocky crests and in treetops. Lightning is truly a danger to be reckoned with, and knowledge of its characteristics may well save you sudden misfortune in the high country.

One of the popular fallacies about lightning is that it never strikes twice in the same place. Despite its reputation for erratic behavior, lightning is actually one of nature's most consistent performers. It will consistently strike, time and again, the tallest object in the vicinity, whether it be an exposed ridge, a mountain summit or a sizable tree.

Lightning can be defined, in layman's language, as a very long spark of enormous voltage, caused by a strong electrical charge within a cloud which seeks to ground itself. Actually there are three varieties of lightning: (1) within a cloud, or from cloud to cloud; (2) upward stroke, from ground to cloud; and (3) down stroke, from cloud to ground. The first two

---

West from Taboose Pass

forms, although exceedingly powerful and dangerous, are usually no threat to hikers unless they are caught on a mountaintop or in the clouds. The third variety, the down stroke, is the most frequent cause of death and injury to hikers during an electrical storm.

If you find yourself caught in a Sierra thunderstorm, a few simple but very important precautions can greatly enhance your chances of surviving the tempest in good health.

Thunderstorms usually travel at speeds in excess of 25 miles per hour, so it is useless to attempt to outrun one. Your time is much better spent in searching for a safe, dry place to wait it out. You can judge fairly accurately how much time you have by counting the seconds between flash and thunder: a five-second interval means the storm is about one mile away, 2½ seconds indicate a half mile, etc.

The best place to seek shelter is in a stand of small trees or in a shallow depression, away from exposed high points. If you are caught in the open, your ideal body position is crouching low on your knees or haunches with your feet close together. Separate yourself from metal objects, such as tent poles or an ice axe. It is considered advisable by some experts to place at least four inches of insulation between you and the ground, such as a coiled rope or rolled sleeping bag. Stay clear of wet cliffs and shallow caves.

The most dangerous place to be during an electrical storm is high on a mountain. Obviously, descend before the storm hits if you have time; if not, seek shelter in a depression between two flat boulders or, if you can find one, in a deep cave. Under no circumstances should you wait out the storm on a summit, on an exposed ridge or wall, or in a shallow cave.

You may experience a strange phenomenon called St. Elmo's fire, when the head of an ice axe begins to glow, or be aware of a buzzing sound from metal objects such as pitons or carabiners in contact with one another. In either event, separate yourself from the metal objects immediately, as they are conductors and will tend to attract lightning.

Most lightning-caused casualties do not result from direct hits. More often, they result from a radial diffusion of the lightning's voltage through the ground in what is known as step voltage. When lightning strikes, it sends out a charge in an expanding and slowly dissipating circle. The shock you receive depends on how close you are to the strike and whether or not the ground upon which you are standing is a good conductor.

Injuries caused by lightning range from burns, lacerations and contusions to amnesia, paralysis and internal damage. Broken bones and head injuries often result from falls after being struck. Many lightning fatalities are caused not so much by burns and injuries as by heart and breath stoppage induced by electric shock. Artificial respiration in the form of heart massage and mouth-to-mouth resuscitation undertaken immediately could probably save many of these lives. Your chances of surviving a lightning strike are favorable, as, according to the American Alpine Club's Safety Committee, 70% of those struck by lightning recover.

If you use common sense, take the precautions listed above, and come prepared with poncho, tarp and tube tent, there is no reason why you too, like Muir, should not find joy in the refreshing rain, the wild exuberance of light and motion, of a Sierra summer thunderstorm.

The Trails

AN ABUNDANCE OF WELL-traveled footpaths laces *Mt. Pinchot* country, and there are many good trailless routes for cross-country travel. This guidebook describes all the major and most of the secondary trails that cross this central part of the High Sierra, plus a number of trailless routes that the writer considers ideal for backpack travel. All the routes in this book were walked by the writer or his associates, most of them during the summer of 1973.

The hiking routes contained in this guide have, for the purposes of organization and ready reference, been listed generally north to south and separated into three categories: main trails, secondary trails and cross-country routes. The most important footpath described is the famous John Muir Trail, which traverses the *Mt. Pinchot* quadrangle from Upper Basin in the north to Bubbs Creek in the south. Other main trails covered are the Woods Creek, Onion Valley/Kearsarge Pass and Bubbs Creek pathways. The secondary trails, scattered throughout the quadrangle, include three long, steep eastside approach routes—Taboose Pass, Sawmill Pass and Baxter Pass. These secondary footpaths are secondary in usage only; along them, the scenery is fully equal if not superior to the scenery along the major routes. Cross-country routes offer access to many of the delightful high-mountain basins and canyons not reached by trail, and provide lateral connections between established trails.

A word of caution: although most of the trails are well maintained and plainly marked, many of the secondary trails are not. Some of the cross-country routes involve miles of rock scrambling and boulder hopping, and much elevation gain

---

Mt. Clarence King from Muir Trail *Tom Ross*

and loss. It may take all day to traverse what appears to be a short distance on the map. Allow plenty of time, and study this book and its topo map carefully. It is the writer's earnest desire that this little book will provide the prospective High Sierra visitor with the knowledge that can make an outing in *Mt. Pinchot* country an enjoyable and meaningful experience. If you learn and heed government regulations, follow route directions, become familiar with the area, have proper equipment and use good sense, you will thoroughly appreciate your intimacy with the mountains. Never leave the trailhead without this preparation. The Sierra Nevada is no place to travel alone, unbriefed, ill equipped or in poor condition. Enter its portals with the enthusiasm of adventure tempered with respect, forethought and common sense. The mountains belong to those who are wise as well as willing.

THE TRAILHEADS

Because *Mt. Pinchot* country lies along the eastern flank of the Sierra Nevada, the most ready access is from the east, via roads climbing out of Owens Valley. The eastern trailheads are listed below, north to south.

Taboose Creek: Reached by a poor dirt road that leaves U.S. 395 12 miles south of Big Pine, or 15.5 miles north of Independence. Go west, passing Taboose Campground and going right at a fork at 1.7 miles. Pass through a gate at 2.4 miles, and continue to road's end at 5.8 miles. The Taboose Pass Trail starts up the slight rise just north of road's end.

Sawmill Creek: Reached by a poor dirt road that leaves U.S. 395 18 miles south of Big Pine, or 9.5 miles north of Independence. Proceed west on Black Rock Spring Road 1 mile to a junction. Turn right (north) and follow Old U.S. 395 0.2 mile to an unmarked dirt road leading left (west). Pass through a gate and follow this poor road to its end just north of Sawmill Creek, 2.3 miles. The trail starts up an open slope to the northwest (it does *not* follow Sawmill Creek). An alternative, 1.5 miles longer by trail, is to start from Division Creek Powerhouse, reached by a dirt road leading west from Old U.S. 395 1 mile north of Sawmill Creek Road.

Oak Creek: Reached by a good dirt road from Mt. Whitney Fish Hatchery. Leave U.S. 395 2.3 miles north of Independence. Go west on Fish Hatchery Road, the lower part of which is paved, passing the fish hatchery on the right, to a "Y" junction at 1.3 miles. Go right, passing Oak Creek Campground, to road's end at 5.8 miles. The Oak Creek (Baxter Pass) Trail leads southwest, up-canyon just north of the creek, from road's end.

Onion Valley: Reached by an excellent paved road from Independence. Turn west on Market Street in the center of Independence and continue up the road to its end in Onion Valley, 15 miles. Kearsarge Pass, Golden Trout Lake and Robinson Lake trails start from here.

The standard westside approach to the *Mt. Pinchot* quadrangle is via the Cedar Grove roadhead in Kings Canyon, then on foot up the Paradise Valley/Woods Creek Trail or the Bubbs Creek Trail. For details, see the High Sierra Hiking Guide to *Marion Peak.*

Trail Descriptions

MAIN TRAIL #1

The John Muir Trail

The John Muir Trail follows essentially a high route, close under the Sierra crest, through the *Mt. Pinchot* quadrangle. Southward, the famous footpath enters the region in Upper Basin, crosses the South Fork of the Kings, climbs over Pinchot Pass, drops down Woods Creek, ascends its South Fork to beautiful Rae Lakes, climbs over Glen Pass, and descends to Bubbs Creek—30.5 inspiring miles of mostly timberline and above-timberline rambling. Because the country is so magnificent, you are likely to encounter numerous hikers, and many of the campsites are overused. The National Park Service has asked backpackers to 1) use already established campsites, 2) use stoves for cooking and limit your wood fires, 3) camp only one night in overused areas, such as the Rae Lakes, 4) avoid polluting streams with detergents and garbage and 5) carry out what you bring in. Without these conservation practices, the heavily used Muir Trail would soon lose its great appeal.

Leaving the *Big Pine* quadrangle (see the High Sierra Hiking Guide to *Mt. Goddard*), the Muir Trail enters *Mt. Pinchot* country in Upper Basin, alongside the headwaters of the South Fork of the Kings. It descends the gradually sloping granite amphitheater just west of the creek, passing alternately through

lodgepole forest and verdant grassland dotted with wildflowers,
including purple aster, alpine buttercup, Indian paintbrush and
lupine. Looming high to your right are the impressive granite
spurs of Mt. Ruskin; to your left are the darkish talus slopes
leading up to Cardinal Mountain. You pass a fine lodgepole-
canopied campsite beside the creek, and just beyond reach a
junction with the Taboose Pass Trail. A quarter mile farther
southwest is the unmarked junction with the Cartridge Pass
Trail, descending right. Go left, as indicated by a sign *Pinchot
Pass 4.5*. After a short descent through dense lodgepole forest,
you pass another fine campsite and reach the turbulent South
Fork of the Kings River. Cross via some well-placed boulders
and a log just downstream from the trail.

Here you start the long climb to Pinchot Pass. The trail
turns southeast and climbs through bouldery terrain to another
stream crossing, flanked by another good campsite. Beyond,
your footpath leads steeply upward in a series of short switchbacks that climb out of the glaciated trench of the South Fork.
You make a long upward traverse south-southwest, then climb
steeply to a junction with the higher fork of the Taboose Pass
Trail. You cross a small creek of churning white water and
emerge from the forest into lush grassland. About 100 yards
beyond the crossing is the unmarked trail leading west to
Bench Lake. Continuing south, your pathway climbs through
meadows and clumps of lodgepole, passing above a shimmer-
ing lakelet on the left, then another on the right. Gnarled
whitebark pines, harbingers of approaching timberline, begin
to replace the lodgepoles as the forest thins to scattered groves.
After skirting another rockbound lake, your granite-floored
trail climbs to the north shore of magnificent Lake Marjorie.

Many small campsites hide among the dwarf whitebark pines that border the lake. The setting here is as richly colorful as any in the Sierra: to your right, ramparts of steel-gray granite rise abruptly from the lake. South, above the lake's head, are slopes of black and ruddy brown. Just visible on the southeast skyline is the dark notch of Pinchot Pass. To your left, rising above all, are the broken, multihued cliffs of Mt. Pinchot. The geologic story written in the rocks here bears testimony to the complexity of the Sierra's formation.

The Muir Trail skirts the east shore of Lake Marjorie and climbs above the last, stunted whitebarks into the world of snow and bare rock. You ascend steadily over granite benches and through boulder fields, passing above two stark lakelets. After fording an icy rivulet, the path switchbacks steeply up over rocky terrain to 12,110-foot Pinchot Pass, on the divide that separates the waters of the Kings' South Fork from its tributary Woods Creek. The views in both directions are inspiring. Far to the north, over Mather Pass, loom the black sentinels of the Palisades. South, beyond the serrated face of Mt. Cedric Wright, ridge after ridge fades into the distance.

The pathway descends a steep talus slope, crosses a slight rise and drops into a high, open basin lush with grass and wildflowers. Particularly abundant are clusters of red heather and shooting star. You veer eastward, passing several placid tarns and fording the twin headwaters of Woods Creek, then turn south again and parallel the vibrant stream through alpine-meadow country. As you descend below 11,000 feet, clumps of whitebark pine welcome you back to timberline. The knife-like peak that dominates the southern skyline is Mt. Clarence King. The trail drops steadily southward, passing a marshy

lakelet on your right. To your left, shaded by whitebarks, is
the first improved campsite since Pinchot Pass, distinguished
by an elaborately built fireplace. Occasionally visible down to
the left are Twin Lakes, nestled close under the spines of Mt.
Cedric Wright. A quarter mile below the lower lake you reach
a junction with the Twin Lakes Trail; good campsites are
located along the west shores of both lakes. A half mile below
the Twin Lakes junction is the unmarked junction with the
Sawmill Pass Trail. (The sign has been removed to discourage
travel over the pass into the bighorn-sheep area.) Here, along
the creek under a canopy of lodgepole, is a fine campsite.

Your path veers southwest, ever dropping, following the
U-shaped canyon cut by the glacier that flowed down Woods
Creek. You pass another fine campsite on the left, and when
you abruptly emerge from the forest, the great trough of
Woods Creek opens in full grandeur ahead. For the next 3
miles, the trail descends through the gorge, sometimes alongside the joyous creek but more often well above it, through
tangled thickets of dwarf aspen, willow and other greenery.
Wildflowers add an abundant splash of color, and you may see
Indian paintbrush, larkspur, purple aster, mountain violet,
Bigelow sneezeweed, Labrador tea and yarrow. A ribbon of
white water plunges from the dark cliffs high on your left.
You cross several benches shaded by isolated clusters of lodgepole, then ford the White Fork of Woods Creek, sometimes
difficult in early season when the water runs high. Ahead is
the great bend of Woods Creek, with the stupendous ramparts
of King Spur as a backdrop. A descent over rocky terrain
brings you back into the forest, now consisting of Jeffrey pine
and gnarled junipers. You ford another side stream and drop

alongside Woods Creek, its white froth spilling wildly over huge, inclined granite slabs. On the final descent to the canyon floor, manzanita provides a thick and thorny ground cover, with scattered Jeffreys for shade. At a major trail junction, the fork to the right is the Woods Creek Trail down to Paradise Valley; the Muir Trail goes left. Where you re-reach Woods Creek, it is swollen to river proportions by the addition of its South Fork's waters. There are excellent campsites, shaded by tall aspens and white alders, on both sides of the creek. Overuse has made firewood scarce, and stoves are recommended. Fishing for brook and rainbow trout to 10 inches is fair to good.

You cross the creek via a log with railing, turn southeast and begin the long climb up the South Fork. Juniper and red fir provide forest cover as you pass several adequate campsites on the left, along the creek. Also to your left, half-hidden by foliage, is one of Shorty Lovelace's pigmy log cabins. Shorty ran a trap line through this southeast part of *Mt. Pinchot* country during the years before Kings Canyon National Park was established. Remains of his other miniature cabins are located in Gardiner Basin and along Bubbs Creek. Your trail rounds the base of King Spur and climbs well above the stream, through alternating stretches of lush greenery and wildflowers, and sparse forest of aspen, red fir and lodgepole pine. You jump the rivulet that hurries down from Lake 10,296 and enter an open, rocky area. Beyond, a wooden span provides an easy crossing of a boggy meadow. From the meadow you climb over a rocky ridge and ford the major creek descending from Sixty Lake Basin, passing through a gate in a drift fence. There are several small campsites here, under scattered pines. Across the canyon, Baxter Creek stitches a ribbon of white down the rock-ribbed slope. The trail climbs through rocky terrain, then approaches the main creek, passing a lodgepole-sheltered campsite on the left, before again breaking into the open and ascending bouldery terrain. Ahead looms the peaked monolith of Fin Dome, heralding your approach to the beautiful Rae Lakes. To your right are the impressive steel-gray ramparts of King Spur. In contrast, the massive, sloping Sierra crest in the east is made up of darkish metamorphic rocks. The long black striations that cross the face of Diamond Peak and the ridge north of it are metamorphosed lava, and thus visual evidence of ancient volcanic activity.

Finally this long ascent climbs over a low, rounded spur and abruptly reaches the northernmost of the Rae Lakes chain, jewellike Dollar Lake. The setting here is magnificent: lodgepoles crowd the shore amid granite outcroppings, and Fin Dome, along with some blackish spires beyond, provides a jagged backdrop for the mirroring blue waters of the lake. Good, though overused, campsites lie on the north and northwest shores. Because of overuse at all the Rae Lakes, no wood fires are allowed and there is a one-day camping limit. The unmarked Baxter Pass Trail takes off northeast from the north side of Dollar Lake. (The trail sign has been removed to discourage travel.)

The Muir Trail skirts the west shore of Dollar Lake, climbs over a granite bench, crosses the inlet creek and ascends gently sloping granite slab and sand above the marshy second lake in this chain. Ahead and to the left, the ebony giants of Painted Lady and Dragon Peak, their faces lined with orange and white bands, provide a colorful and impressive backdrop. The trail climbs southeast, about 100 feet above the two middle Rae Lakes, then crosses a low, forested ridge into a grassy basin. A side trail branches west to a summer ranger station, above the southeast shore of the largest lake. Just beyond, an unmarked footpath branches east to Dragon Lake. Here, several campsites nestle under whitebark pines to your left. The trail turns west and crosses the rocky isthmus separating the middle and upper lakes, passing numerous small campsites. The overuse here is obvious. Once back to the "mainland," you reach a junction with the Sixty Lake Basin Trail, branching west.

The Muir Trail now begins a fairly short, steep ascent to Glen Pass. You leave behind the last, scraggly whitebark pines and once more enter the alpine world of snow and bare rock. A series of short switchbacks takes you out of the Rae Lakes basin and onto a granite bench dotted with sky-blue tarns. You ford their icy outlet stream and cross the austere bench, then zigzag steeply up over very rocky terrain to 11,978-foot Glen Pass, on the divide that separates the waters of Woods Creek from those of Bubbs Creek. As at most High Sierra passes, the view is breathtaking. The skylines both northward and southward contain a profusion of jagged summits, the most impressive sight being the high Kings-Kern Divide in the south.

From the pass your trail switchbacks steeply down over broken-granite terrain, passing a lakelet and several small tarns, then rounds a westward-projecting spur and re-enters forest. As the beautiful glimmering waters of Charlotte Lake appear below, the pathway veers southeast and makes a long, gently sloping descent, through open whitebark and lodgepole stands,

to a junction with a trail to Kearsarge Pass, branching east. A short distance south, at another junction, a lateral trail leads west to Charlotte Lake and a connecting side path goes east to the Kearsarge Pass Trail. On most summer days there are many people in this area, one of the most overused in the Sierra.

You cross gravelly clearings between groves of lodgepole and foxtail pine, then abruptly make a series of short, steep zigzags down to a junction with the Bullfrog Lake Trail, branching northeast. Bullfrog Lake is closed to camping, because of past overuse. Your pathway fords a small but tempestuous creek and switchbacks steeply down into the deep, U-shaped trench of Bubbs Creek. Across the canyon, East Vidette Peak looms like a mighty sentinel. You recross the creek, passing a shady campsite 20 yards to the east, and descend via slightly longer switchbacks to a junction with the Bubbs Creek Trail, branching west, just before reaching the heavily forested canyon floor. The Muir Trail turns left (southeast), drops to the valley floor, crosses the outlet creek from Bullfrog Lake and reaches the large campsites in Vidette Meadow. (The topo map calls this region Vidette Meadow, although most of it is heavily forested; the real meadow is several hundred yards downstream.) Rainbow, brook and some brown trout are present in the stream. A summer ranger station is a short distance north of the trail. From Vidette Meadow the Muir Trail climbs gently under a canopy of lodgepoles up the valley of Bubbs Creek, staying well north of the rushing waters. As your trail begins to climb more steeply, you leave *Mt. Pinchot* and enter the *Mt. Whitney* quadrangle (see the High Sierra Hiking Guide to *Mt. Whitney*).

Tarn below Bullfrog Lake *Thomas Winnett*

MAIN TRAIL #2

Woods Creek

Woods Creek, from the junction of its South Fork westward down to Paradise Valley, flows through a great, glaciated
valley in the finest Sierra tradition. On both sides, granite
walls soar skyward to terminate in a progression of domes and
spires– the most awesome being Castle Domes and the north
end of King Spur. Man feels dwarfed by the grandeur of
nature here. A fine, well-traveled trail climbs along the north
side of the valley from the confluence with the South Fork of
the Kings River to a junction with the Muir Trail—part of the
very popular Cedar Grove/Paradise Valley/Woods Creek/Rae
Lakes/Bubbs Creek loop. We describe here the stretch up
Woods Creek from the South Fork ford, just off the *Mt.
Pinchot* quadrangle. (For the trail section between Cedar
Grove and the confluence of the Kings' South Fork and Woods
Creek, see the High Sierra Hiking Guide to *Marion Peak*.) The
entry limit from Cedar Grove is 30 persons per day.

From the ford of the South Fork of the Kings, difficult in
high water, the duff-floored trail leads east, just north of the
rushing waters of Woods Creek, passing several excellent campsites. An abundant forest cover thins out as you climb east.
Where granite walls close in on the raging creek, your trail
ascends the north slope and traverses a hundred feet or more
above the stream. You ford two small tributaries, pass through
a drift fence and descend to Castle Dome Meadow—named for
the colossal cliffs of white granite visible high on your left.
The trail skirts the north edge of the verdant meadow, passing

through clusters of scraggly aspen, to a shadeless campsite at
the east end. A sign indicates *One Day Limit*; the same restric-
tion holds for all campsites along the Rae Lakes loop. Your
trail winds through more dwarf aspen, re-enters forest and resumes its steady climb east. A side trail leading right drops 50
feet to several excellent campsites along the river. You pass
another campsite on a pine-shaded bench, where a sign warns
Poison Forage, and beyond it another drift fence. The trail
climbs onto another forested bench and levels out. You walk
alternately over granite slabs and sandy soil for the final mile
to the John Muir Trail junction. Red fir and lodgepole pine
begin to appear, and, in the last quarter mile, your trail winds
through a beautiful aspen grove, the broadly ovate leaves
whispering in the slightest breeze. From the Muir Trail junction, marked by an abundance of signs pointing north, south
and west, it is 100 yards down to your right to good campsites
along the bubbling creek, under a cool canopy of aspen and
alder. To continue on the Rae Lakes loop, or to travel north
on the Muir Trail, see Main Trail #1.

MAIN TRAIL #3

Kearsarge Pass

Kearsarge Pass is the major eastside gateway to *Mt. Pinchot*
country, and numerous are the hikers who tramp over it every
summer weekend. From road's end in Onion Valley, you gain
2600 feet in 5 easy-graded miles of walking, passing en route
a number of sparkling lakelets, some of them stocked with
rainbow and brook trout. Once over the crest, it is an easy

downhill walk to the sky-blue Kearsarge Lakes, to the Muir Trail, and to Charlotte Lake. This route also offers the shortest trail approach to the immensely popular Rae and Sixty Lake basins.

Heavy use in the last two years has caused the National Park Service to restrict entry over Kearsarge Pass to 60 persons per day. You have a much better chance of gaining entry if you begin your trip on a weekday—Monday through Friday. Weekends are so crowded that rangers have turned back as many as 100 hikers.

Onion Valley—named for the swamp onion that blooms here in July and August—is the starting point for this most popular of *Mt. Pinchot* trails. The pathway, marked by a wooden sign and register box, leaves the road just before the latter turns south to a campground. You climb over sandy, manzanita-covered slopes, making a long switchback leg north, then a leg south, with a few red firs and limber pines for occasional shade. Looking back, you get a breathtaking view, between serrated canyon walls, across Owens Valley to the rounded, tawny crest of the Inyo Mountains. As you zigzag upward through open terrain, just north of tumbling Independence Creek, the granite spine of University Peak looms high on your left. Clusters of timber—mostly lodgepole, with some foxtail pine—begin to appear as you top the long slope and climb onto a mid-mountain bench. The trail crosses a terminal moraine of granite boulders and skirts the north shore of placid, overused Gilbert Lake. Forested campsites with very little wood are at both ends of the lake. Fishing for rainbow and brook trout is good in early season, but the waters here are usually fished out by mid-July. Matlock and

Slim lakes, reached via a short cross-country jaunt across the low spur to the south, offer good angling because of their hidden locations. Just beyond Gilbert Lake is Flower Lake, offering fair fishing prospects in early season. Your gently ascending trail climbs north above Flower Lake, through groves of foxtail and whitebark pines, onto a gravelly bench, then makes a series of short zigzags up a steep wall, with views down upon Heart Lake (reached by a trail-of-sorts from Flower Lake; whitebark-shaded campsites at the east end). Notice how the whitebark trees becomes more gnarled and dwarfed as you gain elevation, until just above Big Pothole Lake they are prostrate, more bush than tree. This hardy pine is the toughest, most weather-resistant in the Sierra, growing in elfin form up to 11,000 feet. You climb north of barren Big Pothole Lake, then make a final, long switchback up shaley terrain to the 11,823-foot pass.

The trail crosses the crest one granite gendarme north of the true low point of Kearsarge Pass. A large wind- and snow-battered sign proclaims the boundary of Kings Canyon National Park. The panorama that abruptly unfolds in the west is awesome: in the foreground are the jagged teeth of the Kearsarge Pinnacles; beyond, the serrated rampart of the Kings-Kern Divide. Below, glimmering in the sunshine, are the Kearsarge Lakes and Bullfrog Lake. The trail drops westward on gravelly footing, switchbacking down the south slope of Mt. Gould. Near timberline you reach a junction with the trail to Kearsarge Lakes and Bullfrog Lake. The main route formerly descended that way, skirting the north shore of Bullfrog Lake. Then, because overuse was seriously threatening the lake and its surrounding terrain, a new trail was constructed that stays high on the slope. Going right at the junction, your route makes a long, gradual descent westward. Down to your left are the usually placid waters of Bullfrog Lake, with the spiked summits of East Vidette and West Vidette across the chasm of Bubbs Creek as a lofty backdrop. Farther south are even taller Junction Peak and Mt. Brewer. Continuing west, the trail makes a "Y" fork: go right here if you intend to travel north on the Muir Trail, left if you are heading west for Charlotte Lake or south on the Muir Trail. Going either way, you reach the Muir Trail in a quarter mile.

The left branch of the trail continues westward, crosses the Muir Trail and then descends via short switchbacks through a cover of lodgepoles to the southeast end of long Charlotte Lake. Numerous campsites are scattered above the northeast shore. Continuing along this shore, you pass a ranger station, 50 feet up to the right. Just past the lake, the maintained trail ends and an unimproved footpath continues west, then north to Gardiner Basin (Secondary Trail #7).

MAIN TRAIL #4

Bubbs Creek

From shining snowfields and sky-blue lakes high under the Sierra crest between Mt. Gould and Junction Peak, silver ribbons of flowing water descend westward and join to become rushing streams, which in turn unite into hurrying creeks of churning, cascading white water. Farther down the slope, these join to become the mighty torrent of Bubbs Creek. Through the ages, this powerful mountain river has carved a deep groove in the Sierra bedrock all the way to its junction with the South Fork of the Kings. In more recent geologic time, glaciers have gouged and widened the chasm into the beautiful U-shaped canyon it is today. Since man has been on the scene, the great canyon has served as an avenue for trans-Sierra travel. Today it is part of the very popular Rae Lakes loop.

Because of this loop's popularity, and to preserve the wilderness values of the region, the National Park Service has been obliged to impose travel restrictions. The entry limit for Bubbs Creek, for those starting from Cedar Grove, is 30 hikers per day. Overnight camping is restricted to one day per party per campsite.

The trail route up Bubbs Creek begins at Cedar Grove (see the High Sierra Hiking Guide to *Marion Peak*). The pathway enters the *Mt. Pinchot* quadrangle at the 7000-foot level and continues its steady ascent above the north bank of the tumultuous creek. You pass a number of fair campsites alongside the stream under a mixture of lodgepole and Jeffrey pine and white fir. High above on the left, the broken cleft of Charlotte Creek's canyon comes into view, guarded over by the granite sentinel of Charlotte Dome (Point 10690 on the topo map). Avalanche chutes line the imposing south wall of the canyon. One feels insignificant amid the titans of nature here, as elsewhere in the glorious High Sierra country. You continue the steady ascent amid modest forest cover, with lodgepole pine becoming increasingly evident. The path steepens during a short, rocky stretch, then resumes its gradual climb up the north side of the great canyon. Stands of water-loving quaking aspen and white alder announce your approach to the verdant clearings of Junction Meadow. Camping and grazing in the meadow itself are now prohibited, to prevent further damage to the grasses and wildflowers. The trail to East Lake and Lake Reflection branches south here (see the High Sierra Hiking Guide to *Mt. Whitney*). Your best camp-sites are beside Bubbs Creek near this side trail.

Continuing east, the trail climbs steeply under a canopy of red fir and some Jeffrey pine. You pass close alongside the thundering rapids where the creek hurtles through a narrow granite chute before dropping to Junction Meadow, then veer away from the tumult of water and climb through thickets of manzanita, chinquapin and sage. A few twisted junipers pro-vide occasional shade. Back to the southwest, you catch a glimpse of Mt. Brewer's granite pyramid above the defile of East Creek. The trail re-enters forest cover, exclusively lodge-pole now, crosses a small tributary creek, and passes several good campsites on the right. You reach another fine camping area at the west end of Vidette Meadow (the topo-map label shows Vidette Meadow too far east) and, a few hundred yards beyond, come to a junction with the John Muir Trail (Main Trail #1).

SECONDARY TRAIL #1

Taboose Pass

The high, broad gap in the Sierra crest called Taboose Pass was crossed by Paiute Indians centuries before the white man arrived. The word *Taboose* is an ancient Paiute word for an edible groundnut still found in the region. The Taboose Pass Trail today is essentially the same as it was in Indian days, the lone difference being modern man's proclivity for making switchbacks up steep grades. (Indians always preferred the direct, no-nonsense route.) This trail is a lengthy, exhausting climb from the floor of Owens Valley (5400′) over the broad 11,400-foot pass and down into the watershed of the South Fork of the Kings River. The expansive views, the delightful flower-bedecked basin just over the pass, and the direct access via this route to the sparkling gem of Bench Lake make the great effort worthwhile *if* you are in top shape.

From the Taboose Creek roadhead you cross a low lateral moraine and ascend gently eastward over a sandy, sage-covered plain, with the awesome rampart of the Sierra—which *you* must climb—just ahead. The path veers left as you enter the broad portal of Taboose Creek canyon and gradually rises, staying above the rushing creek. A small campsite down to the left is shaded by a solitary white fir. You drop momentarily alongside the willow-choked creek, then climb steeply up-canyon on footing alternately gravel and rock. The trail zigzags up a steep slope, passing a handful of lonely Jeffrey pines, then contours over to the creek. Just north of the creek is a clearing ringed by willows, where one can camp. You hop boulders across the creek, taking extreme care not to slip.

The trail switchbacks up through a mini-forest of white fir and a few Jeffrey pines, then crosses a bench with an excellent campsite on the left. Beyond, you climb steadily eastward, once again in the open, through thickets of chinquapin, willow and other greenery. Looming high on your left are the

yellowish-brown spurs of Goodale Mountain. You pass a
small campsite alongside a trickling side stream, then cross
the main creek again and zigzag up around a waterfall, over
bouldery terrain. The trail once again fords the seething creek
and then climbs to a picturesque bench valley, shaded around
the edges by gnarled whitebark pines, and hemmed in between
rust-colored cliffs. Several excellent campsites are under the
whitebarks on the left. The footpath fords the creek for the
fourth time, then switchbacks steeply up through very rocky
terrain to a last bench just east of the pass. You are now well
above timberline, but lush grasses and colorful wildflowers
make the scene delightful. Look for Sierra primrose, alpine
buttercup, shooting star and alpine columbine. You wind up
and between granite outcroppings, passing several limpid tarns,
and finally reach Taboose Pass, marked by a large wooden sign
announcing your entry into Kings Canyon National Park. The
scene that abruptly unfolds is breathtaking. Directly ahead is
the deep crease of the Kings' South Fork. Slightly to the left
is beautiful Bench Lake, with the symmetrical spire of Arrow
Peak as a backdrop. To the right is the ragged citadel of Mt.
Ruskin. And it all looks so close!

Your trail drops southwest down a gradual slope, passing
through sky gardens of buttercup, shooting star and senecio,
carpeted with velvet green. You ford a rivulet, pass just north
of a rockbound tarn, and reach a junction. Straight ahead is
the main trail, which descends steeply through whitebark and
later lodgepole pine, crosses the South Fork of the Kings, and
intersects the John Muir Trail just northwest of the stream.
Branching left is an alternate trail that climbs, then contours
along a rocky slope, staying above the U-shaped bowl of the

South Fork, to a junction with the Muir Trail 100 yards north
of the Bench Lake turnoff. Either route brings you to the
Muir Trail in about 2 miles of walking.

SECONDARY TRAIL #2

Cartridge Pass

From a hot August day in 1895, when Stanford professor
Bolton Coit Brown and his trusty mule Jack struggled across
the bouldery defile of Cartridge Pass, until the completion of
the Muir Trail segment over Mather Pass in 1938, the pass was
a major thoroughfare for High Sierra travelers. Today, the trail
from the Middle Fork of the Kings up over the difficult gap
and steeply down to the Kings' South Fork is still passable,
but it is steep and narrow, and it feels the tramp of few hikers.
It does, however, lead through prime High Sierra country,
particularly the sublime Lake Basin near the headwaters of
Cartridge Creek.

For the stretch from the Kings' Middle Fork up lower
Cartridge Creek into Lake Basin, see the High Sierra Hiking
Guide to *Marion Peak*. The trail enters the *Mt. Pinchot*
quadrangle just as you climb past the last stunted whitebark
pines in upper Lake Basin. You follow Cartridge Creek,
through miniature alpine meadows sprinkled with wildflowers,
then skirt the northeast shore of the barren upper lake.

Immediately above the lake, your trail turns south and
zigzags over rocky and sometimes loose footing up the steep
wall of Cirque Crest. Once above the wall, you ascend a

gradual talus slope to the granite-rimmed gap of Cartridge Pass (11,750′). Southward across the yawning defile of the Kings' South Fork is the much photographed white pyramid of Arrow Peak.

From the pass, the trail drops south over talus and granite slabs, passing a barren lakelet, into a beautiful alpine basin containing two unnamed lakes. It is surprising that this hanging valley and its sky-blue gems is unnamed, for it equals in grandeur many that are. The pathway skirts the eastern shore of the lower lake through a veritable garden of red heather, alpine buttercup, wild onion, shooting star, Indian paintbrush and other flowers, to an excellent campsite near the lower end, where clumps of whitebark and lodgepole pines provide shelter. Continuing south, your route drops into a lodgepole forest just east of the seething creek, then contours east along a granite bench before plunging downward to the floor of the valley on some of the steepest, shortest switchbacks in the Sierra. At the bottom, you intersect the river trail, turn east (upstream) and immediately reach the South Fork of the Kings. The trail crosses the broad flow of water at a foot-wetting ford, parallels the south bank, and three-fourths mile upstream recrosses to the north bank. To avoid this difficult double fording, you can remain on the north bank and work up-canyon through a maze of avalanche-downed trees and across two talus slides.

Beyond the second ford, follow the footpath as it climbs
northeastward, above the river, through lodgepole cover, to
meet the John Muir Trail.

SECONDARY TRAIL #3

Bench Lake

Bench Lake, as its name implies, lies in the lap of a broad,
nearly flat bench a thousand feet above the South Fork of the
Kings. In the clarity of its waters and in its splendid setting
amid granite peaks and spurs, this sparkling jewel is unsur-
passed in *Mt. Pinchot* country. Hikers will appreciate the
short side trip to this sublime mountain lake, less than an
hour's walk off the Muir Trail.

You leave the Muir Trail in a sloping meadow 100 yards
south of the junction of the upper trail to Taboose Pass (unsigned as of August 1973). Your pathway leads west across a
flower-bedecked meadow, descends a short distance, then contours southwest along a granite bench under a canopy of
lodgepole pines. You ford a shallow stream, pass two limpid
tarns, and in 1.5 miles from the John Muir Trail reach the
northeast shore of Bench Lake. The whitish pyramid of Arrow
Peak, reflected in the lake's mirrorlike waters, is one of the
classic views in the Sierra. Many fine campsites are among the
lodgepoles along the north shore. The trail skirts the north
shore and rounds the west end of the lake before fading away.
Halazone tablets are recommended if you drink the water here,
as the campsites alongside the lake are heavily used and the
lake's drainage is gradual.

SECONDARY TRAIL #4

Sawmill Pass

You can begin this long, grueling march from Owens Valley over the Sierra crest from either of two trailheads: Sawmill Creek or Division Creek. The shorter, though steeper, route is from the Sawmill Creek trailhead. The trail from Division Creek, starting just above the powerhouse, climbs a more moderate grade and gives you a close look at a cinder cone rising out of the Sierra foothills. Starting from either point, you face a long, shadeless, waterless, uphill trudge before finally reaching the welcome forest and stream well up Sawmill Creek. Start early in the morning or late in the afternoon, and carry at least one quart canteen. The entry limit is 25 hikers per day.

To avoid the precipitous gorge of lower Sawmill Creek, your route up from Sawmill Creek climbs the steep, sage-covered slope to the north. In early summer, this desert slope is splashed with flowering shrubs and blossoms of bright-blue woolly gilia and yellow and white buckwheat. From the trail you look down on the Big Pine volcanic field, spotted with reddish cinder cones and black lava flows that erupted from the west side of Owens Valley. After a lengthy switchback, your trail rounds Sawmill Point high above the tempestuous waters of Sawmill Creek, visible as a white ribbon far below. The pathway descends slightly, then contours, and finally climbs along the precipitous north wall of Sawmill Creek canyon. Jeffrey pines and white firs make a most welcome appearance as you near the sloping ridge known appropri-

ately as The Hogsback. If you look carefully at the lower end
of The Hogsback, you can spot the remains of the Blackrock
Sawmill and flume, dating from the 1860s, after which Sawmill Creek and Sawmill Pass are named. For some distance
above The Hogsback, you can occasionally spot stumps, felled
trees and logs used as "gliders" in this century-old operation
to supply Owens Valley miners with lumber.

The trail climbs to meet a tributary stream north of The
Hogsback, and here is your first water and a fair campsite
under pine and fir. You ford the small creek and zigzag
steeply up the north slope of The Hogsback. Once over the
top of this long, rounded ridge, the path veers south, contouring and climbing on a moderate grade back into the main
canyon, and reaches Sawmill Meadow, boggy and lush green
in early summer, but drying considerably as the summer
months progress. Good campsites are located on the north
and northwest flanks of the meadow. Beyond, the trail follows the creek, then zigzags steeply upward through Jeffrey
pine and red fir to swampy Mule Lake, perched on a small
bench high up the canyon. You ford the creek and climb
through a jumbled mass of metamorphic rocks, home for a
large colony of conies. Listen for their sharp, nasal bleeting.
After recrossing the creek, you arrive at the northeast shore
of beautiful Sawmill Lake. Superb campsites under clumps of
foxtail pine are located here, and fishing for rainbow trout is
fair to good.

Above the lake, your trail winds upward through a thinning
forest of foxtail and whitebark pine, crosses a small timberline
basin, and climbs steeply upward to Sawmill Pass (11,347'),
on the border of Kings Canyon National Park. From the pass

you walk northwest across nearly level talus and sand, then drop into a resplendent lake-dotted alpine basin, clothed with whitebark pine, verdant meadows and wildflowers—the head-waters of Woods Creek. The trail winds westward, gradually descending as it passes just north of two small, nameless lakes. Superb lodgepole-shaded campsites are located on both sides of the pathway. The largest body of water in the basin—Woods Lake—is a short cross-country jaunt south of the trail. Your route descends to the lower end of the basin, then turns abruptly north, climbing and contouring along the lower slopes of Mt. Cedric Wright. Finally, your trail drops to the North Fork of Woods Creek, goes north along its east bank a short distance, and then fords the creek to a junction with the John Muir Trail.

SECONDARY TRAIL #5

Baxter Pass

The trail over 12,300-foot Baxter Pass is the highest in the *Mt. Pinchot* quadrangle, and you start your foot-slogging journey just above the floor of Owens Valley, at 6000 feet. Needless to say, it is a long, grueling trek, and it should be attempted only by hikers in excellent physical condition. Because the trail passes through the bighorn-sheep area, it receives only minimal maintenance. (Downed trees may be removed and rock slides worked over, but that's all.) The trail does have unique features, however. It is the only one of the four trails over the crest in the *Mt. Pinchot* quadrangle that

---

does not have a long shadeless stretch at its beginning. And, where it crosses the crest, it passes through a strange, utterly desolate waste of black, brown, orangish and rust-colored metamorphosed rock, a landscape more befitting the moon than the earth. Entry limit is 25 hikers per day.

The trail begins at an oak-shaded campsite at road's end on the North Fork of Oak Creek. You proceed up the canyon, on the north side of the creek, following an old dirt roadway. Where the old road forks, go right, and soon begin climbing via trail, through sagebrush and scattered clumps of wild-flowers—buckwheat, mountain mint, lupine and paintbrush. The trail enters a grove of Jeffrey pine spotted with oak and some pinyon pine, fords a small tributary stream, and a short distance later crosses Oak Creek via a log to a large, oak-shaded campsite. You now begin to climb in earnest. The trail ascends a sage-covered slope, then strains upward around a rib of lichen-stained rock. You re-enter forest cover—Jeffrey pine and red and white fir—ford a trickling side creek, and once again cross the North Fork, this time without the benefit of a bridge. The trail now zigzags up the canyon floor through a thick mantle of sage, manzanita and chinquapin, with occa-sional firs for shade. Purplish lupine and Indian paintbrush of several hues add splashes of color. You climb more steeply and reach a forested bench incorrectly identified as Summit Mead-ow on the topo map. A large packer campsite is located about 200 yards to the left. Continuing up-canyon, you twice swing to the right to get around rock obstructions, passing small campsites along the creek. Above a glaciated bench, the trail negotiates a ledge-and-crack labyrinth before reaching the alpine basin in which lies the real Summit Meadow, so signed.

Heather, grasses and stunted lodgepole and whitebark pines proclaim your approach to timberline. A good campsite lies along the edge of the grassy clearing, the last campsite before Baxter Pass. This upper part of the North Fork canyon slices down through a 2-mile-wide mass of pregranitic, meta-morphosed rocks, rust-hued and greenish-tinged, streaked with black. Altogether, the scene bears little resemblance to the predominantly granitic parts of the High Sierra.

From Summit Meadow the trail ascends through dwarf stands of whitebark pine and patches of bright shooting star, penstemon and Labrador tea, then veers north and switch-backs steeply up to barren Baxter Pass (12,300'), on the eastern boundary of Kings Canyon National Park. From the pass, your trail negotiates a steep slope, then winds through a desolate, lunarlike little valley of black, gray and ruddy-hued rock before descending, again steeply, to the largest and high-est of the Baxter Lakes.

You skirt the north shore of this timberline lake through alpine grasses laced with colorful shooting star, heather and buttercup, cross a verdant meadow, and pass some campsites protected by clumps of hardy whitebark pine. The trail now descends westward, a few hundred yards north of Baxter Creek and its several shining lakelets, passing a number of fine campsites. You ford a small tributary, then cross the main creek just below the outlet of another small lake. The trail descends more steeply as Baxter Creek begins its final plunge into the South Fork of Woods Creek. Then, abruptly, your route climbs around a bouldery prominence through a grove of foxtail pine, and contours south high above the South Fork. The jagged white peaks of the King Spur dominate the

skyline to the west, and ahead, above the glimmering jewel of
Dollar Lake, looms Fin Dome. The trail finally drops steeply,
fords the South Fork immediately below the outlet of Dollar
Lake, lowest of the Rae Lakes, and joins the John Muir Trail
at an unsigned junction.

SECONDARY TRAIL #6

Sixty Lake Basin

The sapphire pools and lakes of Sixty Lake Basin, strung
together like beads on the silver ribbons of their nourishing
streams, are a delight to behold. Lodged as precious gems
between the granite rampart of the King Spur on one side and
the Fin Dome ridge on the other, they are excelled in natural
charm by few other lake chains in the Sierra. Access is easy—
only 2 miles by trail from Rae Lakes—and angling for rainbow and brook trout is good in early season, though only fair
as the summer progresses. Unfortunately, overuse in recent
years has scarred some of the trailside campsites, but the dili-
gent explorer can still find isolated nooks near lakes not
touched by the main path. Stoves are recommended for cooking, as downed wood is scarce. There is a one-day camping
limit per campsite.

You leave the Muir Trail at the northwest edge of the
uppermost of the Rae Lakes, where a sign points west to *Sixty
Lake Basin 2*. The path has been rerouted around the north
edge of a small meadow dotted with lupine, shooting star,
paintbrush and aster. Once beyond this grassland, you climb

steeply over granite outcroppings, the home of numerous marmots and conies, contour north through a sparse pine forest, ford an icy rivulet, and switchback to the top of the ridge just south of the soaring granite monolith called Fin Dome. Your trail skirts the shore of a fishy lakelet surprisingly situated almost on the ridgetop, then zigzags steeply down on rocky footing to the first of the Sixty Lakes. There is a fair campsite among whitebarks here. You ford the small outlet creek and then sidehill down into the basin proper, passing a superb but overused campsite to your right. Sixty Lake Basin, as you now witness, is anything but flat; it is a conglomeration of crystal-blue lakes and tarns, each on a different level, separated by granite ridges, slabs and outcroppings, and dotted with golden-brown whitebark pines, lodgepole pines and a profusion of alpine flowers, all of it lorded over by the cloud-piercing spines of Mounts Cotter and Clarence King: truly an enchanted and serene place to while away your wilderness vacation. The main trail threads northwestward around and over the uneven terrain, passing close by several lakes and tarns, then turns north and descends into the lower part of the basin, finally fading away along the east shore of the northernmost large lake. Small campsites are numerous along both sides of the trail. A profusion of faint fishermen's paths—sometimes difficult to make out, but the cross-country is easy—lead to the lakes of the upper basin to the south.

A short route back to the lower Rae Lakes follows a barely distinguishable trail northeast from where the trail north down the basin crosses the 10,720-foot contour. The route leads northeast through a little pass and then curves east to the shore of Arrowhead Lake (not named on the map).

SECONDARY TRAIL #7

Gardiner Basin

If you value serenity and relative seclusion amid true alpine surroundings, and are tired of encountering the swarms of hikers and campers who crowd the Muir Trail and other popular routes in the Sierra, visit Gardiner Basin. This hidden sanctuary, forested in its lower reaches and spotted with sparkling lakes, ringed on three sides by granite ridges and sharp peaks, will satisfy your longing for a genuine wilderness experience. Only a handful of hikers reach this isolated basin, because only one footpath, seldom maintained, enters it, making the long climb from Charlotte Lake over Gardiner Pass. It is one of the few areas in *Mt. Pinchot* country reachable by trail where the marks of man are minimal.

From the west end of Charlotte Lake, the trail fords Charlotte Creek and skirts the south edge of a grassy clearing, passes some excellent campsites under lodgepole pines, and crosses again to the north side of the creek. Beyond here, as a sign indicates, the trail is infrequently maintained. You cross a maze of avalanche-downed trees and descend westward, above the stream, through a mixed forest of aspen, lodgepole and some juniper, punctuated with clumps of manzanita. The trail drops gradually along the south slope of Gardiner Ridge, leaving the rapidly descending creek far below. Ahead is the Yosemitelike monolith of Charlotte Dome, unnamed on the map but strikingly prominent. Finally you begin climbing through an open forest, cross a low rocky spur, and reach the bubbling North Fork of Charlotte Creek (not named on the topo map). Your trail recrosses the creek twice, passing a fine lodgepole-shaded campsite 50 yards to your right after the second ford, traverses a small meadow and commences the long climb to Gardiner Pass. The trail makes numerous switchbacks during its lengthy ascent, through a fine forest of lodgepole pine, with tall foxtail pines becoming predominant as you near 11,000 feet. From the 11,200-foot pass—one of the few forested passes over 11,000 feet in the Sierra—breathtaking panoramas open to the north and south. To the south, the high rugged summits of the Kings-Kern Divide lace the sky. Northward, you look over the deep trench of Gardiner Basin to peaks as far north as Mt. Goddard.

From Gardiner Pass your trail zigzags steeply down into the glaciated head of Gardiner Creek's South Fork, fords the icy creek, and reaches an unnamed lake. Good campsites are located on a granite slab at the lake's northwest end, and 100 yards down the trail below the lake. For the next 2 miles, you descend from granite bench to granite bench, arranged like progressive stepping-stones, several of them harboring tarns or marshy lakes. The forest cover becomes exclusively lodgepole, interspaced with verdant clearings laced with colorful wildflowers. The trail passes 50 feet above the east edge of the lower lake, then drops to a superb campsite along the northeast shore. From here, you cross a low rise, then abruptly drop in unbelievably steep zigzags to the floor of Gardiner Creek's main basin. To your left, hidden in forest and brush on a small flat 200 yards south of the creek, is the remains of one of Shorty Lovelace's pigmy cabins, built in the years when Shorty ran a trap line before the establishment of Kings Canyon National Park. Beyond this point, the topo map

shows a footpath ascending eastward into upper Gardiner
Basin. But it would violate the writer's sense of propriety to
call this a trail. It is nothing but a ducked route, with occasional semblances of trail, that climbs through brush and over
boulders and granite slabs to Lake 11,394 at the upper end of
the basin. The route is described in this book as part of Cross-
Country Route #6.

SECONDARY TRAIL #8

Parker Lakes

The isolated, barren Parker Lakes lie close under the jagged,
dark cliffs of the Sierra crest just southeast of Black Mountain.
Because the lakes are within the summer range of the bighorn
sheep, entry is restricted from June to October. To visit these
lakes during the summer months, you must obtain written per-
mission from the Lone Pine office of Inyo National Forest.

The route begins 8 miles up the Onion Valley Road from
Independence, where a dirt side road leads north, blocked by
a locked gate. Be sure not to block the gate when you park.
On foot, follow the dirt road as it contours north along the
sage-covered Sierra slope. After crossing the tumbling waters
of Sardine Creek, you reach a road junction. Continue north,
rounding the slope into Little Onion Valley. Now on-trail, you
ford the small South Fork of Oak Creek, then veer left and
begin the long climb up the canyon. You walk alternately
through brush and sparse forest cover of Jeffrey pine and red
fir, passing by a small campsite to your left near the head of
Little Onion Valley. The trail steepens, fords a small tributary

creek, and finally zigzags up to the outlet of lower Parker Lake. Just below the outlet is another small campsite. The upper lake is a quarter-mile rock scramble up the canyon.

SECONDARY TRAIL #9

Sardine Lake

Tiny Sardine Lake, tucked under immense talus slopes near the head of an ancient glacial cirque, almost never sees hikers. Set amid stark surroundings, and barren of trout, the little lake does not rank among the gems of the Sierra. Nevertheless, if you're looking for a one-day conditioner, and if you relish off-the-beaten-track solitude, this hike should appeal to you.

Your hike begins the same as Secondary Trail #8. Upon crossing Sardine Creek and reaching the road junction just beyond, go left and follow the poor dirt road, then the trail, as it climbs steeply up Sardine canyon. The trail has not been maintained in recent years, and may be difficult to follow in some places. You cross and recross the tiny creek a number of times as the path zigzags up to the rocky bowl in which lies Sardine Lake.

SECONDARY TRAIL #10

Golden Trout Lake

Crystal-blue Golden Trout Lake, named for the famous fish that have been planted in its waters in recent years, lies in a picturesque alpine setting, close under the great talus slopes and rocky spurs of Mt. Gould and the adjacent Sierra crest. The trail to this sparkling jewel is a popular day trip out from the Onion Valley roadhead. A superb campsite at the lake makes this a pleasant overnighter too.

You have a choice of beginning routes. You can take the wide, rocky path that leads northwest from behind and just east of the Onion Valley store, or you can follow the main Kearsarge Pass Trail to near the end of its first long switchback leg, then bear right a few yards on the packer's trail, then go left onto the first-mentioned footpath. Using either approach route, you are soon heading northwest toward the thin white ribbon of Golden Trout Fall, clearly visible above. You ford the small creek, then climb very steeply, over rock that is sometimes loose, just east of the waterfall. The trail here is seldom maintained; watch your step. Once above the fall, you enter a sparsely wooded area, cross the creek, and climb eastward over bouldery terrain. Where the canyon narrows, continue straight, avoiding a side trail that drops to the creek. Your trail finally descends to the creek, fords it, and a short distance beyond refords to the south-facing slope. After 2.5 miles from the trailhead you reach a lush meadow spotted with rivulets and small tarns. Your trail skirts the south edge of this marshy meadow, then bears left through a grove of splendid, gnarled whitebark pines. (The topo map shows a trail ascending the north fork of Golden Trout Creek to two other unnamed lakes. This old footpath has not been worked in recent years; however, the route is easy cross-country, and the lakes, close under the face of Dragon Peak, are well worth visiting.) From the meadow you climb among whitebarks and a few foxtail pines up the small canyon, south of the creek, then wind more steeply up to the outlet of Golden Trout Lake. There's a beautiful campsite among golden-brown whitebark pines along the lake's eastern shore.

SECONDARY TRAIL #11

Robinson Lake

This is a short, delightful day hike from Onion Valley up into the glacier-carved bowl between Independence Peak and the spiny northeast spur of University Peak. The small, oval gem of Robinson Lake lies as a delicate sapphire amid bold alpine surroundings. Although it is less than 2 miles from pavement and campground, you get the feeling of true wilderness here, and the nourishment thus afforded should revitalize you.

Your trail begins at the east end of the Onion Valley Campground, just beyond road's end. You pass through a thicket of dwarf aspen, ford a small but vibrant stream, and begin a gradual climb eastward up the brushy slope. After negotiating a few gentle switchbacks, the trail tops a sloping bench and turns south. For the next mile you climb steadily, mostly on rocky footing, with occasional lodgepole and foxtail pines for cover, up into a U-shaped basin ringed on three sides by awesome granite walls and talus slopes. Finally you surmount a slight bouldery rise and reach the outlet of Robinson Lake. Several fine campsites lie under foxtail pines along the west shore of the lake.

SECONDARY TRAIL #12

Kearsarge Lakes, Bullfrog Lake

The beautiful Kearsarge Lakes lie just over Kearsarge Pass, tucked in against the dense array of steep spires called Kearsarge Pinnacles. The lakes' great popularity with backpackers has resulted in severe overuse, and now the National Park Service has been obliged to restrict camping here to one night and, in order to save what forest is left, to prohibit wood fires. Damage from chronic overuse has been so bad at Bullfrog Lake, 1 mile northwest of the Kearsarge Lakes, that camping at Bullfrog has been prohibited indefinitely. To discourage travel to Bullfrog Lake, the main trail from Onion Valley has been rerouted high on the slope to the north. The old footpath, skirting the north shore of the lake, offers a scenic shortcut route from Kearsarge Pass to Bubbs Creek.

You leave the main trail 0.6 mile west of Kearsarge Pass, going left at a junction signed *Kearsarge Lakes*, and descending the gravelly slope to the basin floor just north of the lakes. Here you reach another junction. Going left (south), the trail crosses the granite basin, through sparse clumps of whitebark pine, to the north shore of the largest Kearsarge Lake. Numerous campsites are scattered in both directions along the lakes, reached by well-beaten fishermen's paths. Proceeding right (west) at the before-mentioned junction, you descend a gently sloping high valley to Bullfrog Lake. The trail skirts the north shore, with grand views southward across the Bubbs Creek trench to the towering pyramid of East Vidette. You cross a forested rise, walk through a marshy meadow and past

---

a limpid tarn, re-enter lodgepole forest, and reach a junction with the Muir Trail just before the latter begins its steep zig-zag down into Bubbs Creek canyon. A fine campsite is located just left of this junction, the closest one to Bullfrog Lake.

CROSS-COUNTRY ROUTE #1

Vennacher Col

This prominent gap immediately south of Vennacher Needle provides a direct route for knapsackers between Upper Basin and Lake Basin. The going is easy except for one 100-foot Class 3 pitch on the west side of the col. Hikers not accustomed to Class 3 may want a rope belay over this pitch.

Leave the Muir Trail in Upper Basin, where it crosses an unnamed tributary due east of Mt. Ruskin. Proceed up along-side a southeast-flowing creek over bouldery terrain, staying to the right of a prominent granite spur, to an unnamed lake basin. Continue northwest up a series of granite benches—delightful walking—to Vennacher Col (12,360'), the gap clearly visible on the skyline just south of Vennacher Needle, actually more of a pyramid than a needle.

The west side of the col is very steep for the first 100 feet. It is best to descend westward from a point about 125 feet north of the actual low point. You drop in precipitous fashion (Class 3) for about 100 feet before the grade eases as you descend a steep chute full of small talus and coarse de-composed granite. Below this, the going is easy as you drop

into a granite basin dotted with tarns. Proceed southwest over
bouldery terrain as you descend alongside a creek to a junction
with the Cartridge Creek Trail in Lake Basin.

CROSS-COUNTRY ROUTE #2

Muro Blanco

Muro Blanco, meaning "White Wall" in Spanish, actually
refers to the great serrated cliffs southeast of the South Fork
of the Kings River, extending from Arrow Peak to the defile of
Woods Creek. But to hikers, *Muro Blanco* means the canyon
itself. Hemmed in on the southeast by the walls of Muro
Blanco and Arrow Ridge, and on the northwest by the broken
ramparts of Cirque Crest, laced with churning rapids and cas-
cades, this majestic gorge drops almost 3000 feet in 7 rough
miles. What's more, it is one of the few great canyons of the
High Sierra that is trailless. Numerous backpackers have
descended the length of Muro Blanco, but this is no jaunt for
the beginner, nor for anyone not well versed in cross-country
travel. For 7 miles you work your way down boulder slopes,
cross loose talus, traverse granite slabs right next to the roaring
creek and, worst of all, beat your way through fierce thickets
of brush. Although the effort is slow and painstaking, the re-
ward is a genuine wilderness experience. Nature reigns supreme
here; man is the intruder. You should feel as John Muir must
have felt a century ago.

The route here is described going down the Muro Blanco,
much the easier direction to travel. (Beating downhill through

brush is bad enough; working uphill through it is next to impossible!) The description begins where the trail from Cartridge Pass meets the South Fork of the Kings (see Secondary Trail #2). For the first mile, you follow a trail just above the north bank of the river. The trail disappears as you cross a boulder field, then reappears for the last time as you enter a grove of lodgepoles. An excellent campsite is located within the grove, to your left alongside the river. The trail disappears for good as you cross a grassy area, then enter a dense thicket of dwarf aspen. Over the next 4 miles, you alternately fight through brush and traverse boulder slopes, passing isolated stands of lodgepole pine containing fair campsites. Although the opposite (southeast) bank occasionally looks easier going, stay on the northwest side all the way down to avoid difficult and dangerous fords of the rampaging white water.

The going is rough, but the canyon scenery is superb. Wildflowers carpet the river banks; look for lupine, larkspur, paintbrush, yarrow, leopard lily and groundsel. Rivulets trickle and splash down from enormous side slopes as the great gorge gradually veers southward. A large grove of lodgepoles four miles down offers welcome rest and a superb campsite. Beyond, you resume your struggle with dense thickets—predominantly willow, chinquapin and manzanita—and cross boulder fields. Sometimes you have a choice of staying in brush close to the river or traversing boulders and talus high above. After fording Kid Creek and fighting down through more dense brush, you reach a welcome area of granite slabs containing several good campsites, shaded by ponderosa pine, incense-cedar and white fir. Below this, you struggle through the most horrible brush in the canyon before dropping to the forested floor a half mile short of the South Fork's junction with Woods Creek. This final half mile through ponderosa pine and incense-cedar is a veritable paradise when compared with what you've been through. In the forest you pick up a faint trail that soon becomes more distinct, pass several shady campsites on your left alongside the now-placid river, and reach a junction with the Paradise Valley Trail opposite the confluence of Woods Creek.

CROSS-COUNTRY ROUTE #3

Arrow Pass

Arrow Pass, unnamed on the topo map but well known to climbers, is the rocky gap three-fourths mile southeast of Arrow Peak. Although it lies well away from established trails, the pass was once used by sheepmen—to drive their herds from Paradise Valley to Upper Basin. Today, knapsackers occasionally use it as a shortcut between Bench Lake and Paradise Valley or Woods Creek.

From the west end of Bench Lake, contour southwest through a lodgepole forest and over granite outcroppings to the unnamed creek east of Arrow Peak. Ascend the creek a short distance to the unnamed lakelet at its head, then climb southwest over talus to Arrow Pass (11,650′), the gap on the skyline. Drop west, then south to the lake at the head of Arrow Creek. Descend the creek all the way to its junction with the South Fork of the Kings, just north of the confluence of Woods Creek. It's easy going until the final mile, where Arrow Creek drops steeply to the South Fork; descend the east side of the falls, negotiating a short pitch of Class 3.

An easier alternative is to leave Arrow Creek where it makes its westward turn just below the third lake, climb south over the southwest spur of Pyramid Peak, then descend south to a creek and follow its east bank down to the Woods Creek Trail.

CROSS-COUNTRY ROUTE #4

Explorer Pass

Like Arrow Pass, 1.5 miles northwest, Explorer Pass is not labeled on the topo map but is familiar to climbers. Using this steep saddle, you can travel a shortcut route between Bench Lake and upper Woods Creek, visiting the beautiful unnamed lake just east of Window Peak.

The route from Bench Lake to the unnamed lakelet in the basin east of Arrow Peak is the same as in Cross-Country Route #3. Then, from the lakelet, ascend southeast to the head of the basin. Climb steeply up a chute, which usually contains hard snow until midsummer (ice axe advised), to Explorer Pass (12,200'). The climbing is easier if you stay on the slope to the east and gain the pass about 75 feet above (east of) the low point. Descend south, then southeast into the rocky basin east of Pyramid Peak, passing east of the three unnamed lakes, then follow the creek south to the large lake east of Window Peak. There are fine campsites in the forest near this lake's northeastern edge. Turn southeast, passing another small lake, and descend along its outlet creek, steeply down through brush at times, to the Muir Trail above Woods Creek.

CROSS-COUNTRY ROUTE #5

King Col

King Col, the granite-rimmed gap one mile west of Mt. Clarence King, offers a steep but direct route between Woods Creek and Gardiner Basin.

Your major problem is crossing Woods Creek, exceedingly difficult in times of high water. If the creek is low, ford it at Castle Dome Meadow (signed though unlabeled on the topo map); if it is running high, cross 1.5 miles east via the Muir Trail log bridge and skirt the south bank of Woods Creek west to a point opposite Castle Dome Meadow. Proceed south along the west side of an unnamed tributary creek, climbing steeply, through forest predominantly lodgepole pine, into a beautiful glaciated valley. You pass the west shores of three lakes near the valley head, then climb steeply on sand and coarse decomposed granite to the obvious gap one third of a mile west of Peak 11,870, known to climbers as King Col (11,650'). Descend southwest over easy slopes of granite sand, then steeply south into Gardiner Basin to a junction with Cross-Country Route #6.

CROSS-COUNTRY ROUTE #6

Sixty Lake Col, Gardiner Basin

Although thousands of hikers walk the Rae Lakes loop every summer, making a complete circle around Gardiner Basin, few of them ever climb over the intervening ridges to visit this hidden sanctuary of sky-blue lakes, singing creeks and granite spurs. Perhaps this is just as well, for the beautiful basin would lose much of its primeval appeal were it more frequently sampled by the increasing swarms of Sierra hikers. This route penetrates Gardiner Basin from the east, via the low granite gap at the south end of King Spur known as Sixty Lake Col. You can make a delightful round trip through this basin, leaving via Gardiner Pass (Secondary Trail #7) or King Col (Cross-Country Route #5).

Leave the Sixty Lake Basin Trail where it makes its abrupt turn north and proceed southwest, following a faint fishermen's trail, to the west bay of a long, unnamed lake. Climb over granite outcroppings above its west shore toward the prominent gap on the right skyline. As you near this saddle, you may find the ducked route that climbs via granite ledges to the crest of the divide about 200 yards north of the low point. This was once a stock route, and you will occasionally find remnants of the old trail. From the divide, known as Sixty Lake Col (11,700'), follow the ducked route northwest, down an intricate route that threads granite boulders and ledges, to the east shore of Lake 11,394, the largest lake in Gardiner Basin, and on around the north shore of this barren lake. Before reaching the outlet, your ducked route climbs north over a low ridge and drops steeply into a small three-lake basin. From the outlet of this basin, it descends steeply to a tree-ringed lake. To your left, near the lake's north edge, is a campsite, the first since this route left Sixty Lake Basin. Here you begin a steady descent northwest, staying well above the next large lake. (There are excellent campsites on the northwest shore of this unnamed lake, reached by making a short detour left.) Continue down over granite benches, through a forest, staying well above the creek to avoid dropoffs, to the unnamed creek that rushes down from the basin southwest of Mt. Clarence King. Cross the creek and follow the ducked route down to Gardiner Creek at a point just north of a marshy lake. You ford Gardiner Creek and pass a superb campsite, then contour west over granite slabs to avoid another dropoff, to a side creek descending from a lake-filled basin to the south. Your ducked route fords this side creek, then zigzags steeply down to Gardiner Creek, follows close to its south bank for half a mile, then climbs left. You cross another granite bench, then drop southwest, away from the creek, crossing a boulder and brush area, to a small forested bench on which lies, half-hidden, one of Shorty Lovelace's old pigmy cabins. Here your ducked route becomes a trail, which zigzags steeply south toward the basin below Gardiner Pass (see Secondary Trail #7).

CROSS-COUNTRY ROUTE #7

Dragon Pass

Dragon Pass, a 12,800-foot notch in the Sierra crest halfway between Dragon Peak and Mt. Gould, provides a shortcut, one-day route between Onion Valley and Rae Lakes. Don't attempt this route unless you are well experienced in cross-country travel; it involves much boulder scrambling and a very steep, ankle-twisting descent over loose talus.

There are two ways to reach Dragon Pass from the trailhead in Onion Valley.

The most direct is to take Secondary Trail #10 to Golden Trout Lake, then climb east and north over boulders and talus to the small notch a half mile north of Mt. Gould.

Slightly longer but more on-trail is a route that follows the standard trail to Kearsarge Pass, then climbs north cross-country up the granitic rib of Mt. Gould, circles west around the summit, and continues north along the sloping plateau just east of the crest to Dragon Pass.

The most difficult part of the trip is the descent, first down a steep chute over very loose talus, then over boulders, from Dragon Pass to the easternmost of the three unnamed lakes south of Dragon Lake. From this barren lake, proceed north over bouldery terrain to Dragon Lake, then down the trail from the lake's north shore to a junction with the John Muir Trail just east of Rae Lakes.

An alternative, even more direct route but one involving Class 2+ scrambling, is to cross the Sierra crest via the 12,500-foot notch half a mile north of Dragon Peak called by climbers North Dragon Pass. Take Secondary Trail #10 from Onion Valley toward Golden Trout Lake, but turn right at a creek ford before reaching the lake and ascend northwest to the two unnamed lakes that lie just below and east of Dragon Peak. Then climb over boulders and talus toward the notch north of Dragon Peak, but before reaching the notch (which is not your pass) veer north toward a prominent square-topped peak. Traverse around the east side of this peak and continue north, just east of the crest, around a minor summit to North Dragon Pass. Descend northwest, then west on scree to Dragon Lake, where you take the before-mentioned trail down to the Muir Trail just east of Rae Lakes.

CROSS-COUNTRY ROUTE #8

Charlotte Creek

Decades ago a sheepmen's trail ascended Charlotte Creek from Bubbs Creek to Charlotte Lake and beyond. This old path has all but disappeared, although hikers can still find occasional traces of it. Today Charlotte Creek is a genuine cross-country jaunt involving some bushwhacking and rock scrambling. If you're traveling up Bubbs Creek and your destination is Gardiner Basin or Charlotte Lake, this route saves you several miles of walking, but it is rough going with a pack.

The route follows the right bank of Charlotte Creek all the way up. You encounter some brush lower down, and negotiate several pitches of steep rock scrambling where the creek passes through its defile above Bubbs Creek canyon; some may wish a belay here. Once above the defile, the going is an easy walk through forest and grassland, with occasional brush, all the way to the junction with the Gardiner Pass Trail 1 mile east of Charlotte Lake. If you're heading for Gardiner Basin, the most direct route is to turn north, along the tributary creek just east of Charlotte Dome, and follow it up to the trail. This route is brushy in spots. Longer but easier is to continue up Charlotte Creek another three quarters of a mile, then climb steeply north to intersect the Gardiner Pass Trail.

Climbers

CLIMBING A MOUNTAIN CAN BE an exhilarating and rewarding experience—providing one is in good physical shape, stays within his capabilities, and knows the route. Not only is the climb itself an enjoyable experience, but the view from the summit gives the climber a fresh perspective of the country he is visiting. Nature's pattern of the canyons, the peaks, and the ridges becomes readily evident, and the master plan of the range becomes an integrated whole.

Mountaineers rate climbs in categories 1 to 6, depending upon technical difficulty, not distance involved. Class 1 is a walk and 2 is a scramble; both of these easy categories should provide no problem for an experienced hiker not versed in technical climbing technique. Class 3 is a steep rock scramble requiring the use of both legs and arms, usually with some exposure (the possibility of falling far enough to be badly injured or killed). This category requires some cross-country experience, but not necessarily technical skill, although some people may want a rope belay when doing Class 3. Class 4 requires a rope, and Classes 5 and 6 require one or more ropes and climbing hardware; these three categories should under no circumstances be attempted by hikers not well versed in technical climbing skills.

In *Mt. Pinchot* country there are many splendid mountain peaks, on which routes vary from easy Class 2 up to difficult Class 4. The best ones, most of them climbed by this writer, are listed below with short comments. For information about the exact routes, consult *Mountaineer's Guide to the High Sierra*, edited by Hervey Voge and Andrew Smatko (Sierra Club, 1972 edition).

Castle Domes

Class 2: Anyone with cross-country experience.

Vennacher Needle (12,996'): more pyramid than needle; easy from southeast.

Cardinal Mtn. (13,397'): multicolored peak on crest; loose scramble from Taboose Pass.

Striped Mtn. (13,120'): yellow bands on black make this a striking peak; loose scramble from northeast.

Mt. Pinchot (13,495'): crown of *Mt. Pinchot* quadrangle; steep talus climb from southwest.

Mt. Wynne (13,179'): difficult traverse from Mt. Pinchot, but easy from southeast.

Arrow Peak (12,958'): beauty in symmetry; easy from southeast.

Mt. Perkins (12,591'): loose and steep from west; good views.

Colosseum Mtn. (12,450'): scree scramble up steep chute from southwest.

Mt. Baxter (13,125'): dominates central *Mt. Pinchot* quadrangle; easiest from Baxter Lakes.

Diamond Peak (13,126'): Rae Lakes sparkle like diamonds from here; talus climb from west or southeast.

Black Mtn. (13,289'): highest in southern half of quadrangle; steep scramble up talus chutes from Dragon Lake.

Mt. Gould (13,005'): maximum view for minimum effort; less than an hour from Kearsarge Pass.

Kearsarge Peak (12,598'): gold and silver bonanza on its slopes a century ago, remnants still there; day climb from Onion Valley.

Independence Peak (11,744'): boulder scramble from Robinson Basin.

Class 3: For those with cross-country experience and no fear of heights.

  Mt. Ruskin (12,920'): splendid pyramid of pale granite; breathtaking climb along east ridge.

  Pyramid Peak (12,777'): airy, knife-edge climb from south or northeast.

  Fin Dome (11,693'): guardian of Rae Lakes; granite ledge climb from west, Class 4 from any other direction.

  Dragon Peak (12,995'): metamorphic giant; airy summit block climb from south.

Class 4: For technical rock climbers only.

  Mt. Clarence King (12,905'): one of most beautiful spires in Sierra; climb from south, through hole and over great inclined granite slabs.

  Mt. Gardiner (12,907'): sheer-walled monarch overlooking Gardiner Basin; difficult ridge traverse from south-southeast.

  Kearsarge Pinnacles (12,000+'): near-vertical spires; favorites of rock climbers.

Mt. Clarence King from the east   *Tom Ross*

BIBLIOGRAPHY

There are literally hundreds of books, pamphlets and articles that deal in some way with the *Mt. Pinchot* region of the Sierra Nevada. The ones of greatest benefit to the reader and prospective hiker are listed below.

Bowen, Ezra. *The High Sierra.* New York: Time-Life Books, 1972.

Brewer, William H. (ed. Francis P. Farquhar). *Up and Down California.* Berkeley: Univ. of California Press, 1966.

Brown, Vinson, and Robert Livezey. *The Sierra Nevadan Wildlife Region.* Healdsburg, Calif.: Naturegraph Co., 1962.

Chalfant, W.A. *The Story of Inyo.* Bishop: Chalfant Press, 1933.

De Decker, Mary. *Mines of the Eastern Sierra.* Glendale: La Siesta Press, 1966.

Farquhar, Francis P. *Place Names of the High Sierra.* San Francisco: Sierra Club, 1926.

_____. *History of the Sierra Nevada.* Berkeley: Univ. of California Press, 1965.

Johnston, Verna R. *Sierra Nevada.* Boston: Houghton Mifflin Co., 1970.

Moore, James G. *Geology of the Mount Pinchot Quadrangle, Southern Sierra Nevada California.* Washington: United States Geological Survey, 1963.

Muir, John (ed. David Brower). *Gentle Wilderness: The Sierra Nevada.* New York: Sierra Club-Ballantine Books, 1968.

Munz, Philip A. *California Mountain Wildflowers.* Berkeley: Univ. of California Press, 1963.

Author on summit of Mt. Pinchot

Peattie, Roderick (ed.). *The Sierra Nevada: The Range of Light.* New York: Vanguard Press, 1947.

Roth, Hal. *Pathway in the Sky: The Story of the John Muir Trail.* Berkeley: Howell-North Books, 1965.

Starr, Walter A., Jr. *Guide to the John Muir Trail and the High Sierra Region.* San Francisco: Sierra Club, 1968.

Stocking, Stephen K., and Jack A. Rockwell. *Wildflowers of Sequoia and Kings Canyon National Parks.* Three Rivers, Calif.: Sequoia Natural History Association, 1969.

Storer, Tracy, and Robert Usinger. *Sierra Nevada Natural History.* Berkeley: Univ. of California Press, 1963.

Sudworth, George B. *Forest Trees of the Pacific Slope.* New York: Dover Publications (reprint), 1967.

Voge, Hervey, and Andrew Smatko. *Mountaineers Guide to the High Sierra.* San Francisco: Sierra Club, 1972.

Webster, Paul. *The Mighty Sierra: Portrait of a Mountain World.* Palo Alto: American West Publishing Co., 1972.

Zwinger, Ann H., and Beatrice E. Willard. *Land Above the Trees: A Guide to American Alpine Tundra.* New York: Harper and Row, 1972.

Related Wilderness Press Publications

Schumacher, Genny. *Deepest Valley: Guide to California's Owens Valley*, 1969.

Schwenke, Karl, and Thomas Winnett. *Sierra South: 100 Back-Country Trips in California's Sierra,* 1968.

Winnett, Thomas, *et al. The Pacific Crest Trail, Vol. 1: California*, 1973.

plus *High Sierra Hiking Guides* to the adjacent map quadrangles of *Marion Peak, Mt. Goddard* and *Mt. Whitney.*

Index